SMUTCUTTER: HOW I SURVIVED PORN

SMUTCUTTER: HOW I SURVIVED PORN

By

Madison Premo

Aka

Sonny Malone

BearManor Media

2024

DEDICATION

To my wife,
I dedicate this book
In its entirety
Believing it to be of all my works
The least unworthy of one
Without whose encouragement, sympathy,
And Criticism
I could never have become even
Such a writer as I am.
-    John Galsworthy to his Ada
-    And me to my B*

ACKNOWLEDGMENTS

When they say it takes a village, I am lucky to have that village around me. That village was filled with encouragement, excitement for this journey, and endless hands to help me up when I fell down.

Dana B., thanks for being the first to read and shape this book from my brain. I cannot thank you enough for being there all those times I had my late-night office breakdowns.

Ben S., my savior, and a true hero. You will never know how much you helped with the completion of this book and all my writing. You provided the instrument for which I was able to play and create. Thank you, Captain.

Thomas and Rae, thank you for the endless support and bottles of excellent wine. You two are the best cheerleaders any creative person could have. Your friendship is something we treasure.

Monopole Wine in Pasadena, CA. Thank you to Patty and Lucy for letting me spread out over multiple tables while Rae refilled my Prosecco.

PROLOGUE

I have seen more pornographic movies than your average frat house. I've seen things that I will never unsee in my next lifetime. For some reason, when I entered the Adult Industry, the thought that I would see more adult material than was humanly possible never crossed my mind. I was going to be editing and creating but still be home by 5 p.m. I wasn't going to be constrained by the insane hours of mainstream post-production which usually included eighteen-hour days, often six days a week. I insisted on having my cake and eating too; a career in editing and a home life. But, here is the main drawback to my former life: Law and Order.

Yes, the television show. Here is why. When I used to mainline Law and Order (to watch Jerry Orbach because he was totally awesome) my mind would go beyond the plot down a disturbing back alley. The detectives would sit down with the grieving widow or widower in a windowed conference room with metal Venetian blinds in the middle of the precinct. People outside of the windows were busy running around, shuffling papers as the spouse wept and blubbered about 'how could this happen'. As the investigation went on, you found out the spouse had a friend who was super close to them and their dead partner and they were questioned next. All parties were wide-eyed and innocent of course and almost always the opposite sex. Then you would see the spouse and close friend in a doorway, very close, muttering. Maybe his hand would slide too slowly up the woman's arm or her hand would linger too long on the man's jaw. It was just a touch, a gesture that showed they had been intimate. The lawyer saw it as a break in the case as the camera zoomed into the particular gesture. What did I see?

I saw the actors naked and having graphic, close-up, sex. Like genitals connecting and boobs bouncing and everything. It would only be a flash in my head but I would see the entire scene to completion. Of course, I had never seen the actors naked but my mind would put them into a scene I had edited but with the lighting and trappings of the show I was watching. I couldn't stop my treacherous brain and the image would flash a few times during the episode until the final 'created by Dick Wolf' came onscreen. Now that I am semi-retired, thankfully, that has faded. But for years, sex was all I saw all around me.

No, never pictured Jerry Orbach naked.

I say semi-retired because no matter what this industry has put me through, I am very reluctant to truly let go. My opinions haven't changed, the only difference is now I am saying them out loud. Or rather, in print.

Let me say upfront, some directors, I feel, take their work far too seriously. What they don't understand is that you are filming people having sex. Not raising the Titanic. I get the allure of wanting to create something interesting but it's just the cellophane noisy wrapper around the candy inside. It's often too loud and annoying and you can't wait to get through it to get to the sweet peppermint stripes inside. This is why the gonzo genre worked so well. No script. Point the camera at a hot girl. She strips. She has sex. BOOM. End of story. For all the directors that are making high art, or think they are, most of your customers are fast-forwarding all that pain-staking awkward dialogue you spent countless hours filming and you spent weeks torturing your editor to get the scene just right by your standards. Then you only spent one hour filming the sex to get the job done for the day. Your priorities are all wrong. When I would show this sort of 'dude, it's a porn film' attitude, I was met with wide eyes, a gasp, and a true clutch-the-pearls moment. How DARE I talk about their precious fuck film as if it wasn't Gone With The Wind. Nope, but it will be gone into the $1.99 bin by next month. Then forgotten by the next movie in the series. You cannot seriously think that Busty Boobs #3 is going to outshine Busty Boobs #147.

We have an expression in porn that no one will admit to in interviews or on a red carpet. It's 'polishing a turd'. Many producers say it under their breath late at night when a two-sex scene shoot day has gone on for over ten hours. I often polished that turd to a high gloss shine and was happily making that wrapper glitter. Editing the actual sex was cookie-cutter and rather boring and the formula has never changed. Never will. The 'acting' was the fun part for me. It was like putting together a one-hundred-piece puzzle with only eighty pieces and no picture on the box for reference so it was always a challenge. If I edited decent acting performances, it often wasn't the actor. It was me. I made one starlet's intake of breath and 'well' before each line go away so she looked stellar. I made a long-lost look from a male actor as he rubbed his pants look like he was thinking something profound about his life, his future. Instead of trying to get hard to fuck a girl he wasn't into but had to get paid.

How am I wrong here? I'm asking.

When I told my parents I had left porn (or it had left me, more on that later) and moved to a mainstream job they both said the same thing:

"Oh, thank God."

Not because of the subject matter, but because of the way people had always treated me. I tried to explain that their treatment was often my fault but it was pointed out to me the many times it was not. I was this weird talkative fly buzzing in everyone's ear and trying to be their friend.

Now, I am in a tech company with hundreds of different personalities and somehow, I have had the best conversations over coffee or at my desk with my co-workers. I still hear myself apologizing for talking too much or babbling on and I am ALWAYS told 'No, it's actually fascinating! Tell me more!' followed by real questions because they were listening and truly cared. I feel like I walked through the looking glass backward.

The sweetest conversation was over reheated lunches in the office kitchen. I was talking about my many hobbies and how I am getting back into video games and how my partner and I have been together for close to 30 years. The girl I was talking to was 25. She had the brightest smile as she said: "Your life is so exciting. I can't wait to see what happens to me!" Her enthusiasm for life, hers especially, made my day. It also was the spark to start this book

This was simply me trying to understand who I am outside of porn. It really is a thing. I often felt small and silly. I wasn't a performer or director so I was disposable. I also made sure I lived with a certain amount of excitement: had to be on the set, the parties and award shows, and familiarity with pseudo-celebrities. But I also lived with an insane amount of stress. Freelance will do that to a person, in general. Deadlines are your life and critiques can be personal. Or feel like it. When you edit something it becomes yours and your personal work. When you send something for approval and that nose gets wrinkled and the eyes roll with a huff because you haven't captured their vision, I would crumble easily. Vision? Um.. vision. It's three naked girls playing in a hot tub. What vision did you want there, Scorsese? It's lit right, you can hear and you can see everything. Not to mention, the person who will be watching it will be done with it in about ten minutes (and I think I am being generous). Yes, I have made features I am proud of and many more that I am not. I have remembered just about every scene I've edited over 27 years and there are some clunkers. Many were nominated. Many won and many lost. All were jacked off too. All.

CHAPTER ONE

Yes, adult films do need to be edited. But the most common question I was asked when I mentioned my profession?

"What do you cut out of a porn film?"

I've heard that question for years. Let us get the logistics of the way.

What is cut from an adult film is everything that eludes to real life. Porn is a fantasy and the last thing you want to see are any unwanted bodily fluids or super bad acting to pull you out of the dream. The other thing to note is that the sex scene the viewer sees ends up being on average about twenty-five to thirty minutes. I've cut that from an hour or more of raw footage. You take out the part where the sweat got into the actor's eyes or the false eyelash went south and stayed on the guy's dick during the blow job (total boner killer). You take out the seven false dialogue starts where the actors get the lines wrong. You take out when someone's phone rings because they forgot to turn it off. You take out when that person takes the phone call, all sweaty and out of breath. "Can I call you back?"

I was fairly innocent when I got into the adult business and editing sex just never occurred to me. I was hired to do it, of course, but the actual cutting of it was daunting in the beginning. Also, it hasn't changed in 25 years. I got used to seeing naked people quickly and saw the filming pattern fall into place. Kissing, oral sex, three positions, money shot. End of scene. It was all, and still is very much a formula. It has never and will never change.

To start, I had to make every actor or actress believable. The problem is many of them are great at sex but not so great at delivering lines. As dialogue is sometimes important to move a story along, I learned to read an actor's 'tell'. If you play poker, you will know what that means. If you don't, then a 'tell' is an unconscious action some-one does that indicates they are trying to hide something. In this case, they are hiding the fact that they forgot their lines. Or they forgot that being in a porn film often involves saying a line or two and not just sex. Guys are easy. Their eyes just travel to the girl's boobs. He mutters the line while reaching or grabbing one and we are good. Rarely is the line redone. Girls have it much harder.

One particular actress, a popular one, a very statuesque and stunning blonde, had the 'lip smack and inhale', usually along with a shrugged shoulder. Before *every* line, her eyes would roam over the set in about a five-foot radius as the other actor/actress waited (they knew they had to wait) as she smacked her lips, inhaled sharply, and said 'Well, you know' and then delivered the line. That's what you cut out of a porn film to make the actress look as good as possible.

Other girl's tells are the hair twirl, the giggle, and the 'oh honey' before the line is spoken. They might also swivel on their feet. Much like putting a five-year-old in an office chair, they move constantly. God forbid you put them in an actual office or a place with props! It's like dangling keys in front of a baby, they have to touch and play with everything. They think they look alluring or sexy or it's as if they are actually thinking as they reposition the pen, the lamp, the books, or swivel in the chair back and forth like a windshield wiper. Often, if the girl was new or particularly bad, the director just cut the lines or gave them to someone else. You can have the greatest script ever but if the studio says you HAVE to use their contract girl and she can't act her way out of a wet paper bag, you trim the lines. The other trick is to film the girl's lines one by one by a single cam-era. Then you can just drop the wooden words in where they belong then smash cut to the lunged forward, tongue out heavy sloppy kiss.

That's my favorite. Heavy dialogue that really means something, maybe even something heavy like death.

Male Actor: "Gee, Katelyn (Kirsten, Keersten, Crunchy, who knew!), so sorry your husband is dead." Hand on cock, staring at boobs.

Female Actress, you have to use because she is going to be on the box: "Yes, it's sad." Girl reaches for something on the kitchen counter. She moves an orange three inches slowly, seductively.

Male Actor: "If there is anything I can do… " Guys stops and reaches for her boob. She is on him like a lamprey.

Tongue dive. Tonsil hockey. Naked in seconds. Even though this is the first time the 'characters' are supposed to be having sex, they really seem to know each other's bodies and how they like to have sex since they have been in hundreds of scenes together long before this. The oranges roll to the floor.

Then there is the Mouthy Director. These are the ones I know are pervs in their private life. When a director actually directs, it's for the benefit of the shot. They speak clearly and loud enough for all to hear.

"Move your leg."

"Get your hair out of your eyes."

"Move that stuffed unicorn."

But the last thing I want to hear is *you*, breathing heavily, while saying 'oh yea, right there, perfect, don't move, just like that' all during a great shot. Then you get pissy at me because the audio isn't perfect. I had to take some random audio from oranges hitting the floor to cover your wet dream panting.

Many times I wanted to stand up from my computer, get in the car, track down said director and kick him right in the goddamned balls. Note to all directors: Shut the fuck up.

Remember: Time, Quality, Price. You will only ever get two. If you give me a video with your voice all over it, it is going to take me some time and it won't be the best quality.

Now, on to the gross stuff.

I want to include this because I have had too many (male) people approach me to say 'I just want to cut porn on the side. It will be easy'. Know what I say to that?

Fuck you. Fuck all of you.

This is where the old saying comes in: 'If it was easy, everyone would do it'. I still get texts, emails, and random Instagram DMs asking how to break into editing porn. If you have to ask me, I already know you will never do it once you see your first boob, jack off, and never edit it again. Here is your crash course into the nuances of editing adult films.

First: lack of hard-on. It happens. It's nature. A lack of a little blue pill or a lack of simple chemistry will cause that. Once I had ordered some medication from Thailand (it was simply cheaper!) and as a bonus the company tossed in some of those magic blue pills. I brought them to a set and mentioned I had them.

"You do?" The director looked at me like I was carrying a bottle of Jack with a straw and they were an alcoholic.

"Yeah, I won't use them." I joked as I am female.

"What do you want for them?" They asked. I fought the urge to force them to meet me on the side of the house in the dark. Me in a leather jacket with my hair slicked back, booted heel resting on the wall.

"So, you buyin'?" I would growl over my half-smoked cigarette. They would approach me with wide eyes and a handful of crumpled bills. I'd take the money and shake my head. "Don't get hooked, man. I don't wanna see you back here." Then maybe I would spit.

But, I just handed them over with a smile.

Most guys I've seen are real troopers. If they get paired with someone they are simply not into, somehow they power through. Seriously, I have no problem with most of the men I've edited. Then again, I have edited the best of the best. Amateur stuff has its stumbling blocks but still, 99% of the men I have edited have come through with flying colors. They know they are there to work even though they know it's all about the girl. They know they are basically a dick with a body attached.

Then again, that dick really should be insured. One high-end performer really took one for the team and came back strong. It was in the middle of the scene, the girl was doing what is called a reverse cowgirl. That means the girl is straddling the guy with her back to him. Seems this one new girl was going to town, the guy's hand on her hips. But, she kept lifting off the gentleman too high and came down too hard.

The male performer heard a snap. The whole crew watched him go white. Someone on the set threw up, another passed out. Thankfully he is okay but to this day he can pee around corners.

There were two performers that always got booked to work together and they hated each other! I think it was done just to watch them hate-fuck. When the guy would have issues, she would still help. But she would call him every name in the book as she did it. Their sex was angry. People loved it. It was truly weird.

What is worse is people doing things on camera they do not want to do. Now, I am not saying they are forced at all! They say yes, take the money, and sign the release. They are willing to do these things. I am not talking about anything horrifying here. I am talking about women that do girl-on-girl scenes for the 'easy money'. Also, gentlemen who do not like to service ladies. As I said, no judgment here, everyone has their thing. But there are decent ways to fake things.

When someone does not like to service a lady, you will barely see the tip of a tongue only slightly graze the nether regions of the lady part, then they will start smacking the area like they are flattening a chicken breast for a Milanese. Often fingers are involved but they are inserted so violently it's like they reaching for that lost ring that has fallen down the kitchen drain. The lady on the receiving end of course has to act like this is the greatest thing in the world. When this section of the scene is shot and it is not pleasurable, you will always see the video cut very short. Hands must be washed, false nails retrieved and reapplied, and gentlemen sometimes need a drink. The receiving lady walks like John Wayne after a hard ride to the ladies' room. Yet, the scene is barely over. It is going to be a long day.

Second: razor burn, on the girls. The trend is a clean vaginal area as well as a hair-free anal region. Some of the high-end girls have this done professionally and look abnormally clean, like hair never dared grow there or anywhere! Then you have some of the new girls who just grab a lady Schick or their boyfriend's .99 cent pack of Bic knockoffs on their last leg and go to town. Often the result is a rash and red bumps that resemble poison ivy. Now go back to reason one and you will see my sympathy for the guys.

I want to add something here. Besides the razor burn and not being into the girl, there is the scent. We do have five senses and each performer showers (usually) before a scene so both are clean and not sweaty and ready to go. But with that, you still need some sexual chemistry. If your partner simply has a scent, musk, or sweat or just the way they smell in general, it is going to be a turn-off. Ever been in a crowded elevator on a summer day with no air conditioning? Now, try having sex like that. Yea, it's like that. I've been on the set in a home and have had to step out just to take a deep breath. Sometimes, that funk is thick and hangs in the air like expired Febreze.

Third: fluids that don't belong. Lactation videos, yippee. They are a thing but not my thing. Squirting! Yeah! Know what? No! No judgment, just my opinion here. A director friend of mine was on his knees before two girls dressed in glittery space outfits and having at each other on a foam rock. They were all crammed into a two-car garage along with a lighting guy, an audio guy, and the producer munching popcorn as they watched the two buxom blondes go at it. Had to be one hundred degrees in the small space as the girls went at it right next to a riding lawn mower and a set of golf clubs. One little lady came so hard and let loose so fast that the director had no time to get out of the way thus covering his $6000 camera and himself in personal wetness. Ah, the glamorous life of adult films! When I was editing it, it was like Alien was the liquid spewing right into the very expensive lens and followed by much director cursing and blonde giggling.

Fourth: Sound. Picture two writhing bodies slick with sweat on a pleather couch on laminate floors. After about ten minutes, you can't hear the couple and you want to rip your ears off. You want to kill the dead in the eyes cameraman and crew for not changing the location. Most of them had their faces buried in their phones anyway.

But we're making 'art' here, right? Just checking.

Still want to edit porn? Let me get to the anal stuff.

I've seen it all in all its forms. Performers prepare for anal scenes with enemas. If they are a pro, all usually goes well. If not and they are new… I say, ever been to a Gallagher show? Dig out the poncho and hazmat suit. Again see One. Poor guys and what they have had put upon them, literally.

While we are here let's talk Euro footage. Sure the girls from Budapest are stunning and nearly unbelievably beautiful but they are functioning humans too. Seen it. Up close. Was working for a company that asked me 'Do you edit euro footage?'. Of course, I said, wanting to make sure I kept the job. Besides, how bad could it be? Golden showers, okay, I handled that (barely). Spitting makes me throw up, but I handled it. But when a beautiful brunette squatted on a man's chest and let it rip? I threw up into a nearby trashcan and quit the same day.

Now, everyone has their own thing and I am NOT speaking ill of a person's preferences. You are into what gets your motor going and that's that. I am not judging one bit! All of this is my opinion and my opinion only! Remember that!

As far as just sex, it's not as spontaneous as it seems. Usually, the still photographs are taken first so the couple knows what positions will be covered, and all fluids have been handled, and showers have been taken and tests verified and shared. It's all pretty clinical when you get right down to it. Sure the actors have fun but they are also getting paid for the job they have to perform. A lot of them work with each other often so many conversations before a scene will include talks of daily workouts, how's your mom and yes, my kid started kindergarten.

Edited out are all the times the actors stop because the guy is going soft or the position needs to change because the girl's thigh muscles are twitching and aching or the guy gets a cramp in his foot from trying to keep his hip back to show the complete penetration and action.

The stop and start are what gets removed. Oh, and the director screaming as he is hit with squirting female wetness. That gets edited out too.

CHAPTER TWO

Some of the twists and turns your life takes are rarely planned. One simply has to sit down at the fork in the road and decide which way to go. My mother, stepfather and I moved every year or two for my stepfather's work and I had to adapt. New school, new people, new world. As I got older, I thought that was the way it was. Things happen to you and you just have to take it. It was how I lived until I got into the world of adult films.

I graduated with high marks from film school in Hollywood in the mid-1980s. With a degree in television production and post-production, I struck out into the world to make my way like all bright-eyed graduates. My mother's advice, even after she and my step-father had paid for this expensive education, was to go into accounting for its stability. Naturally, I became a receptionist. But, it was at a multi-stage production facility in the heart of Hollywood with six other working stages across town. A friend who was moving on to other production ventures got me the job. He basically made me his replacement. This made things easy to simply move into the position. Within three months of answering phones, I was moved into the accounting department. Mother was thrilled. I was confused.

Any sort of dream of being in entertainment was indeed perpetuated by working at the studio. But, let me make this clear, the way to production or post-production in Hollywood was NOT through the accounting department. I always slipped down to the lot to see films being made, and peek at celebrities and music stars. Got into trouble more than a few times for leaving my desk for too long. I loved the hours that would pass as I watched costumed actors slip into the large stage doors and into cool blackness. I was once served a steak the size of a car tire off a food truck by Billy Crystal.

I watched Prince and his entourage regally walk to the front gate and out to their cars. Barry Manilow once shot a television special there and at the end of the night, he took my arm and we walked to the front gate, and he ushered in the fans that had been waiting for 12 hours just to get a glimpse of him. He did two songs for these 15 people. Just for them. He was the classiest act I had ever seen.

But, more often than not, I was at my accounting desk far away from the stages. My older female supervisor kept trying to mold me into her image, which was frightening. She was tall with severely bobbed hair and owned horses. An early version of today's 'Karen'. I was in my early 20s and commuting back and forth to Malibu because my mother insisted on a prestigious address. Never mind that I was falling asleep at the wheel on the way home from night school after working a full day at the stages. I moved to Hollywood quickly.

This supervisor had all sorts of advice for me. She would make note of the large bottle of water I was drinking as she passed my desk.

"You know, if you drink one of those a day, anything after is just gravy." She would chirp with a smile, pleased with herself that she had passed on her infinite wisdom. I already hated her. The rest of the female staff had to pretend to like her like I had to pretend. The entire accounting staff, about ten of us, all female.

I was watching my day-to-day life fade into normality that I just didn't want. The rest of the staff was already set with pasted-on smiles and health plans but I was not fitting in. Mom was happy because I had a steady paycheck and was super close to celebrities. She would call daily to ask who I saw on the lot. My mother didn't quite understand how things worked. This is Hollywood with hundreds of productions happening daily all over the city and in substantial sound stages. One day she called me excitedly from her apartment in Toluca Lake and told me there was something being shot at the bookstore down the street.

"All sorts of trucks and lights are set up!" She babbled. I could picture her like Mrs. Kravitz from Bewitched peeking through the curtains and straining her neck to see better.

"Oh cool," I said as I filed yet another folder into a massive metal drawer, staring down at my half-finished bottle of Arrowhead.

"So, what is it?" She asked, perfectly straight. I worked at a major studio. Of course, I should know. Meanwhile, I had a lighting company on hold as I was digging up a check number from the files.

A beat went by and I told her I didn't know.

"But, you work in the industry." She said, nonplussed, and said she was going to walk down and check it out anyway. I told her not to say she had a daughter in the industry. But I knew she would.

It was at this point I realized my mother was pretty much Lucy Ricardo and wanted to be in the spotlight. She wanted to be able to say 'My daughter works in the industry' but required me to have a safe job. I looked around my accounting office filled with filing cabinets and a desk stacked with papers and shivered. I didn't finish my water that day. The supervisor clicked her tongue and shook her head at me.

I had a degree. I was in the wrong place. I quit the same week.

Mom and I had a huge fight about it. I had been an accountant for three years and was going to be just fine on unemployment while I looked for the job I wanted. She wanted to meet Barry Manilow. Mom and I didn't speak for a while.

At the end of my year off, I did take another accounting job at a mainstream production house but I was closer to the inner workings of the place. I could go into the post-production house and into the recording studio and I learned a lot. Also, I promptly got fired for sitting in the post house rather than at my desk. Wow, I really hated desks at this point. Didn't I? There was just so much more excitement in delivering some papers to the post house at 10 p.m. and hanging out while I watched a show being stitched together. The room was dark and soundproof and cut off from the outside world. I could have lived there.

After a few more uneventful jobs I stumbled into a brand new post house that needed a financial officer. It would be only the boss and myself and I said yes. The office had only two rooms and a closet and was the smallest suite in the complex located in the heart of Sherman Oaks. The bathrooms were down the hall and were used by the whole floor. The outside of the place looked like some sort of fairy tale European castle. It was just plain weird. Clearly, it was built by someone who was tired of the standard Russian-looking office block and wanted to get fancy. Every time I pulled into the parking lot I half expected a girl with ridiculously long hair to be calling me from the top spire. The parking was in the middle of the offices on the ground floor so my window looked out to the lot.

After setting up the books I watched as the latest revolution in editing, the AVID, was rolled into the tiny space. I sat in pure awe as it was installed and brought to life. This was the future: non-linear editing.

I had edited in college and fell madly in love with the process. We edited on top loading ¾ decks with a switcher in-between along with a big round dial to move the video back and forth. This was the 80's, kids, ¾ decks were top of the line then. I remember the subject was a long-haired young woman with a pail and small shovel on the seashore digging for clams. Start with a wide shot as she takes two steps. Pail down and lean forward, cutting to close up of the shovel sinking slowly into the sand. Cut to a close-up of the look of concentration on the young woman's face. Editing 101. You are welcome. That will be $5,000.

After only two months, the small post house wasn't doing well and I started to see the real story of the place. A man I will call Wealthy Man purchased this new machine on the advice of the woman who hired me, I shall call her The Mess. Wealthy Man was tall and older and bald but slender and not hideous. The Mess was petite with long dark hair and her eyes never truly focused like she needed glasses but refused to wear them. She always, and I mean always, dressed like Stevie Nicks but wore cowboy boots. Since Wealthy Man wanted to sleep with The Mess, he indulged her with anything she asked. She had me ordering hard drives along with high-end chairs and elaborate window treatments. The new office space was her playground and this guy was just shoveling in as much sand as he could. He seemed to love their little dance. He showered her with gifts and she danced around him like Salome but never put out.

Also, she had several emotional issues that I chose to ignore as I took the job thinking '*she needs me. I can fix her*'. Yes, I was an idiot.

The Mess also had a temper. She would be sweet and light then a switch would get thrown and I swore her eyes turned red. It was like denying a Happy Meal toy to a three-year-old. All smiles then a total terror turned on a dime.

Her husband, yes she was married, had friends in the music industry and they were often invited to concerts and private events. She took me to a local concert at an outdoor theater one night. She had scored some seats to something that was supposedly sold out and the place was packed. We made our way to our seats after getting some drinks, nothing fancy, just wine, when she started.

"Oh wow, these seats are bad!" The Mess whined and pouted. We were about eight rows from the stage. I thought they were terrific.

"I'm so gonna kick someone's ass about this." She said and flopped into the seat, pouting. Her multi-tiered dress fluttered like fallen leaves and draped over both arms of the seat. I sat slowly but kept an eye on her, watching her drink her glass of wine like it was a shot. I waited for her to crumple the plastic cup and throw it on the ground. Maybe wipe her mouth with the back of her hand, trying to be a badass.

The show began and all seemed well. It was an open-air place and as soon as the band started, people lit up and passed some joints around. I skipped that part. The stuff just never did anything for me. I've tried it a few times but I just became 'The Sonny Malone Show'. Ten minutes of rambling stand up, stumbling around then - thud - face down and snoring.

The Mess took a drag and handed the joint back to me and I passed it down. Two girls in their 20s behind us got up to sing and dance. To be fair, the whole place was on its feet, including us eventually. One girl in the back tripped slightly as she was bumped from behind and spilled her drink on us. Like, two drops of her white wine.

"Oh my god! I am so sorry!" She said with wide eyes as she quickly grabbed napkins. We had barely gotten splashed and she was being really apologetic.

"No problem," I said with a smile and helped wipe me and The Mess off. "It - "

I never finished the sentence.

The Mess was on her seat and launching herself at the girl like a tiger. It was like watching Lindsey Lohan in Mean Girls attacking Rachel McAdams over the cafeteria table. I even heard growls.

The girl's friend and I just stood and stared, shocked. She finally spoke first.

"Your friend is beating up my friend!" She yelled.

"She's not my friend, she's my boss," I said. We both watched the others tumble over a few more seats.

"We should… " The girl said.

"Yeah, we should," I said and we finally galvanized to pull the two apart.

The Mess spoke first.

"She hit me! You all saw it! I'm gonna sue you and this whole place! Where is security!? She attacked me!" The Mess was wide-eyed and whipping her head around looking for allies. The other girl was bleeding and had a black eye.

Security eventually escorted all of us out of the venue. The girl's friend and I kept looking at each other as I silently mouthed 'She okay?' and the friend nodded and mouthed 'Thanks'.

The Mess was non-stop angry blathering all the way home. She had been wound up like a toy top and was not stopping.

"I'm gonna sue. I'm gonna put them both in jail. I'm gonna own that whole place. You saw it, you're my witness. We're gonna be rich, man." She said over and over like a mantra.

It was my one and only time in a lawyer's office. I sat for the deposition simply stunned. Did I throw her under the bus and tell the truth or did I lie?

Hold my beer. Honey, I drove the bus and backed up to make sure I got her. The other girls were not even pressing charges and they should have. Yes, I made sure the lawyers knew I heard the words 'We're gonna be rich'.

Obviously, nothing ever came of it and she never knew what I said. Seems frivolous lawsuits for her were like picking up the dry cleaning: routine. I never went out to any event with her again. I had a nice list of reasonable excuses. Including 'I have to wash my hair' and 'I have to shave the cat'. Not a euphemism.

We had a decent roster of clients at the post house and most of them were adult film clients. I realized later that Wealthy Man was part of the Los Angeles fetish community so a lot of his friends were in the adult industry. Hence he was getting us post-production clients. Visits to his home felt like going to a bad haunted house. Lots of red and black leather and whips hanging from the walls. I kept expecting Elvira to pop around the corner and introduce tonight's Bela Lugosi movie. I always wanted to shower after I left the man's home. When we did go, his attention was entirely on The Mess. I was just the driver.

Once, The Mess came into the office asking for the checkbook. She needed clothes for some super high-power meetings that would never materialize.

I pulled out the large book but held it on the desk.

"We don't have any money to spare," I said, softly, gripping the large checkbook.

"But, I need it!" She insisted, whining slightly, hand still out and waiting. "Why don't we have any money? I've been working day and night."

This was wrong. She had been in day and night but had been on the phone arguing with her husband or on the phone talking to Wealthy Man or out running personal errands. I think she was fighting other lawsuits for other fights she had started. She was a multi-tasker.

"But, projects are not done so no money is coming in until they are finished." I reasoned.

Her eyes got large and her face flushed. "I don't have TIME to do all that work!"

"If you don't do the editing, we won't get paid," I said firmly.

"Then YOU do it! I can't handle this!" She said with a flip of her hair and stormed out. After she grabbed the checkbook from my hand.

I sat for a few minutes then leaned my chair back, peeking into the edit bay. Looking over the new machine, I took a deep breath. I have a degree in how to do this, I told myself. Grabbing the manual and the 24-hour tech support phone number, I taught myself how to operate the AVID. I became personal friends with half of the AVID support staff in Tewksbury. Not to mention when an update would arrive, I knew I had made that happen. I was editing porn. It was that simple. No grand gestures or claims to be made, I was editing porn.

Soon, the company was afloat again but I had to edit on the sly. She still took all the credit for the work being done. She seemed to think it was important that Wealthy Man see her as doing everything and I was just a peon. She treated me like that. I was simply to be at her beck and call. I was a slave at Tara and only she could call quittin' time. I worked insane hours to edit around her time at the office to make sure projects got done.

At one point, she finally decided she needed to teach me how to edit. Our clients had nothing but great things to say about the work being done. She hated that. She sat me down at the AVID, talked slowly, and made elaborate movements with her hands like she was teaching a dog a new trick. What she showed me was completely wrong and I tried to tell her I had a degree in this. Also, when the system crashed after she hit several wrong buttons, I got it started again. Thank you, Tewksbury! She said she knew how to do that but wanted to watch me to make sure I knew how to do it. Her editing lesson went on and her reasoning was that I had learned classroom editing and this was the real world.

I fixed every edit she ever did. Still gave her the credit. I was a team player.

The one bitchy thing I want to put in here is when I saw The Mess a few years later. She always thought she was adorable because she was thin and somewhat pretty. She obviously had two men on the hook, so, okay. I was at the AVN trade show when I saw her talking to Nina Hartley. She had filled Nina's head about what a horrible person I was and I never did have a decent relationship with Nina because of it. Which is sad, her husband was a dear and made my first whip; a gray and black leather flogger. Yeah, I said that.

But The Mess at this point? She was wearing the same Stevie Nick's-inspired clothes and cowboy boots but she was fat. Like, my size kinda fat and I'm a size 26.

I call that poetic justice. She was also divorced.

She never did put out to Wealthy Man and he soon tired of the chase. The company only lasted six months. On our last week, I called our clients to tell them of our demise and have a nice day. One company asked who our editor was. They were very pleased with our work and had purchased their own AVID and were looking to hire. When I informed them it was me, they laughed and hired me over the phone on the spot. It was a large porn company I will call Porn Town.

CHAPTER THREE

PornTown was located in the heart of the San Fernando Valley and had just moved to a new facility. It was a large warehouse subdivided into cavernous offices with an attached warehouse for shipping. Basically how all porn companies operate in the Valley; everything under one roof. Like a line from my favorite movie, the day I walked in: "I could still smell the fresh paint."

For the record, it is true about the sheer amount of adult film offices in Valley. A lot of porn offices are in makeshift warehouse spaces. They put all the fancy stuff up front but the back room has as thin as cardboard walls and warehouse space. In the future when I had my own freelance business, I would plan trips to my clients and could see three or four of them in about a two-block radius then hit the Lamplighter on DeSoto and Nordoff for lunch. Which, sadly, now is closed. Great grilled cheese. Great little old-school diner.

The AVID looked tiny in the massive, carpeted space but there it sat. It was three computer screens on a long desk with a second station of tape machines that ran along two-thirds of the back wall of the room. My office was in the center of the collection of offices. The hallway wrapped around my entire space. I could hear if someone from accounting was making their way to the front desk. It was like a wrap-around jogging track at 24 Hour Fitness. We should have charged memberships! The front desk was the best place to eavesdrop as our receptionist was the sister of a high-end mucky mucky at another company. Why he didn't hire her, we never knew. Maybe she was playing spy for her brother? Maybe her brother couldn't stand her? But she talked to everyone like they were her child and she knew absolutely everyone. Also, the company purchased every manner of tape deck for my system that had been invented. However, they neglected to buy a patch bay therefore for every output, I had to rewire every machine by hand. But I am jumping ahead.

The company outfitted the edit hangar with several shelf units along one wall and a large sofa and loveseat, coffee maker, coffee table, several lamps for ambiance, and framed headshots of contract starlets along with covers of magazines that featured the company. All that was missing was turn-down service and a minibar. I had a small closet filled with blank tapes, hard drives, and cables. It was pretty much an editor's dream. It would also be the only edit bay that resembled a mainstream bay I would see in porn. The rest were makeshift closets near the men's room. Again, I jump ahead.

For the first movie I would edit for the company, there was a staff meeting to agree on a title. Yep, you read that right. A staff meeting to decide on a porn title. It was about a real estate office and many of the obvious titles had been used by other companies. We needed something different. Something catchy, something sexy. I watched most of the office file into the meeting but sat quietly in my cavern waiting to be told the new title. There was a soft knock at my opened door.

"Hey, come on." The general manager smiled. "This is a company meeting, we need everyone."

For some reason, I was immensely flattered. I got up, pen and paper in hand, and walked into the packed conference room. People were there from accounting to the warehouse manager. For a little while, it just seemed completely ridiculous to spend this time naming a porn film. But the meeting was very serious; relaxed but serious. There were bottles of water on the table next to a plate of muffins. The furniture was high end and the place looked like any other office with a conference room. I would later find out that every other porn company has the same style of conference room. Everything had to look as mainstream as possible just to prove each company was legit. It would be where mainstream magazine writers looking to interview the owner would be shown and told to wait.

The rooms were always perfectly lit and well appointed yet looked about ten years behind in the decor department. Also, don't look too closely at those chairs. There will be stains.

"The owner will be right with you." A breathy receptionist would utter as she made her way back to the front desk and the ringing phone. She would answer with that same voice.

"Production, how can I help you?" She would say then the person on the other end would identify themselves. Then the receptionist's voice would change to sound like Large Marge from the Pee Wee movie. "Julie, you slut! What's up? Yeah, he's in a meeting. Want me to have him call you? He's giving another interview. I already typed up his answers for him to say."

I should mention something else here. Porn companies never answer the phone with the name of the company. They always have a sweet woman's voice saying 'Production. How can I help you?' God forbid some FBI guy calls and they say the real name.

Phone rings. "Porn R Us, Whaddya want?"

Then it's like that scene from the Blues Brothers with the SWAT team repelling down the building. Hut Hut Hut. But that never happened. Again, I get ahead of myself.

Wow, I really got ahead of myself, let's back up. Naming a porn film in a conference room. Got it. And... go!

After much deliberation, I blurted out the words 'Open House' (not the real title) and the room got quiet.

"Yep, that's it!' The general manager said with a bright smile and patted my shoulder as the room emptied. I still have that VHS.

It was then I met my first real mentor, Frank.

Frank was the general manager. He was an older man with graying hair and large glasses, looking like a Hollywood Agent from an 80's movie. He had a slightly gruff voice from too many cigarettes. He was rather handsome and with all my daddy issues, I instantly fell in love.

At least twice a week, I would hear that soft knock at my door.

"You busy?" He would ask me and smile. I would be up to my elbows in buttholes and boobs and seven outputs to be done before 5 pm.

"Nope." I would smile back as I grabbed my purse and locked the edit bay door behind me.

We were off for three-hour lunches as we picked up sound effects from the local record store to use in the films or he would simply tell me stories about his time in the industry.

One of the best pieces of advice I ever got from him was about my name. Now, I wasn't Sonny Malone yet. I was using a girl's name which really didn't last long. I had a real chip on my shoulder about making sure everyone knew I was a female editor. I had seen females in the offices as the front desk receptionist and in the accounting offices but never in the edit bay. Not even in the warehouse! That was men's work! I was about to use the name Constance MountJoy. Stop giggling.

"Use a name you won't be embarrassed to put on a business card." He said over burnt burgers at the Lamplighter. "Say you are at a cocktail party and someone holds out their hand to say hello. You really want to say: "Hi I'm Constance MountJoy? Only the unimaginative use names like 'Hey, I'm Dick Hard or Betty Blowjob."

He had a point. Hence, I never used Constance MountJoy. For the record, I cobbled that name together from some old movies. It didn't mean what you think it means.

More about how I chose my name later.

Frank became someone very important to me. He looked after me, took care of me, and watched over me. I brought him baked goods and made sure my work was always on time.

The last time I saw Frank was at an AVN show in Las Vegas around 2010. He was ill (heart issues) but getting better and I don't think I ever got the point across of how much he meant to me that first year in porn. How, as a man in this business, he made me feel safe and he was the only one, in twenty-five years, to ever make me feel safe and respected. Not one other person in his position that I ever came across in all those years made me feel that way about myself or my work. He set a standard as to how I thought I should be treated as a professional. That standard was never met again.

An editor from another adult company, a male of course, came in once and I had to help him pick out shots of one of the contract girls for a mainstream interview show. This particular new editor decided that locker room talk was perfectly fine since we were in porn.

"So, you get off in here?" This skinny pimply-faced guy asked, breathing at me like a dirty phone call. He had on a backward baseball hat, a red t-shirt, and baggy jeans. A true fashion plate.

"I'm sorry. What?" I asked, not getting it.

"You jack off in here? This shit get you hot?" He asked, his hand sliding to his crotch. "Cause I do. I go into the bathroom all the time." He was dead serious and I would later find out that 'jacking off' in the bathroom was the norm for young male post-production guys in porn. Made sense why the cardboard edit bays in other companies were near the bathrooms. I was flattered he was treating me like an equal and not coming on to me but this was not the kind of equal treatment I was looking for. This is where I would realize my place. I may have been a female but I didn't look like the girls in the movies therefore I was unfuckable. To him anyway.

I blinked, stood up, and excused myself. I went to Frank's office and closed the door.

"Hey, how normal is this?" I asked. I didn't want to be a crybaby nor did I want to be called an uptight bitch, I just wanted clarification. I explained what had happened and was seeing if I was overreacting. I probably was but this was the first time this was happening and would not be the last.

Frank went slightly pale. "Wait here."

He got up and closed the door when he left. After several minutes he came back in.

"He is gone. Not to return. This is still a place of business and just because we make adult films we still have to follow the guidelines of any company. Sexual harassment included." He said then his eyes softened. "Are you okay?"

I assured him I was and went back into the edit bay. I sprayed the place down the Lysol before I touched another surface. From then on, if the ladies' room was ever being used and I was forced to use the men's… I held it.

The company threw a party to announce the new facility's opening. It would be my first time meeting Ron Jeremy. Our party was in the summer so for some reason we had a baseball theme. The food was hot dogs, popcorn, and other ballpark snacks. The halls and conference room were decorated with baseball-themed streamers and cardboard cutouts of baseballs, bases, and bats. I was nervous about making the rounds to shake hands and was introduced to people as the company's new editor. I was saying my name was Sonny, which is what my friends call me. Often I was met with a polite smile or slight shock that I was female. When I met Ron, he smiled sweetly and held my hand for a moment with both of his. His were cool and soft and his grip was firm but gentle. He was in jeans and a T-shirt and wasn't wearing Crocs yet. Sneakers. He was alert, well groomed, nothing like the man he would turn into. He looked me in the eyes and didn't look away.

"Hi, I'm Ron." He said smiling. "You do know how important you are, I hope."

I merely blushed and all but kicked the dirt with the toe of my shoe.

"No, I mean it." He insisted, still holding my hand, "It's the editor that ultimately makes or breaks a movie. I've heard great things about you. It's really wonderful to meet you." He said, finally letting go of my hand and was whisked away to impress other investors.

I blushed to my ears and never forgot what he said. When I saw him other times down the road, he remembered me. I always took some pride in that.

As I settled into the porn world, I began to see the taboo it held in the real world. I would tell people what I do for work only after I was sure they were my friends or I could trust them. I would see the same thing every time. The eyes would go slightly wide, perhaps a blush would go to the cheeks. Maybe a throat would clear and an adjusting in the seat. Then the questions.

There are two types of people in this world when it comes to porn: only two. The first will instantly slide a hand to a body part, even if they don't know they are doing it, and ask the same questions:

"So, does it make you hot?" Males always ask this with what they think is a seductive smile but it's more like the smile of a creepy clown leaning out of an ice cream truck holding a Rocket Pop.

"Is there sex in your office?" Again, males always ask this and they look me over as if I had just had sex and can they tell.

"Can I get a copy of some movies?" Again, males. This was before the time of free internet porn.

Perhaps a pass would be made as I was suddenly some sort of magical sex unicorn who knew all the sex things. These people I would treat gently. Let them have their fantasy but don't let them within five feet of me again. Unless I was wearing a hazmat suit.

The second has the same physical reaction but they stop themselves and realize I am a person. The questions would then be filled with complete fascination.

"Wow! What do you even cut out of a porn film?" Females ask this one, men too but not as often. If men ask me this, it's them trying to prove they are cool and aloof about this whole sex thing. Or, they were gay.

"Did you go to school for editing?" Female question. Men.. yeah you get the picture.

"How does being a woman doing this sort of work affect you?" Females and two reporters from a German magazine. Male reporters. They didn't make a pass at me. Danke.

I've been interviewed multiple times, including in Forbes Magazine. Each interviewer was respectful, polite, and professional. Even the ones from online adult industry blogs.

Somewhere in here, I decided to try my hand at stand-up comedy on the side. All of this porn fodder just had to be shared. A few friends told me I was funny and I did have an improv background from Second City in Chicago (one crazy summer!) so I decided to give it a shot.

Backing up to Second City for a minute. When I studied improv with Second City, I was just out of high school and living with my mom and stepdad in Lake Point Tower in Downtown Chicago. I had tried a conventional college and lasted only a few semesters at Kent State but quickly found that a continuing formal education was just not for me. Neither was the freshman mistake of an 8am Government class. As I was only 19, in Chicago, I couldn't go to clubs or really be out much on my own in the city alone. Mom found an ad for improv classes and signed me up. It was the most amazing summer of my life. I learned how to listen to an audience, handle being on stage, give and take to my scene partner. When the class concluded, on the last day, the stage manager who was teaching the class took me and one other student to one side, his arms around our shoulders, and said 'You guys are in the traveling troupe, no audition, you are in.' That meant we would be working with the second string of improv comedians on the lower stage, not the main stage. But it was where so many of my idols got their start! I nearly fainted. My dream had always been to be on Saturday Night Live and here was the path! When I got home, the same day, Mom was all smiles when I walked in and said; 'Hey, were moving to California.'

Once I caught my breath, my answer was; 'Go ahead!' I was working enough odd jobs in the building to support myself so I looked for an apartment in town. However, with much pouting and almost begging from my mother and my lack of emotional maturity, I moved with them to Los Angeles.

Once there, I grabbed Variety and looked for more improv classes. If I was good in one place, I would be great here! Imagine my sheer joy when I saw an ad that read 'Second City Alumni teaching improv' with a time and address.

I showed up to the class and instantly knew this was not Chicago. The female teacher had her favorites and I was not one of them. We did not learn technique, stage blocking, or presence. We were to be a breakfast food.

After two hours of pretending to be sizzling bacon, she asked if I wanted to pay $250 per class for the next ten weeks.

I left quickly, but politely.

Instead, I signed up for a stand-up class with a comedy coach who boasted of having taught Whoopi Goldberg! Take my money, please.

In stand-up comedy, I was the Porn Chick. I played the usual places in town: Comedy Store and the Laugh Factory. I never got famous. But I never had to buy my own drinks. Also, never had to book or beg for shows, I was asked and invited to perform a lot. It was fun for a long time until it wasn't. The level of stage fright I developed had me acting like Garbo after I did a set: I want to be alone! But I did have a few jokes that always killed:

The director is on the set and everything is ready but the girl. But since the girls were known for their implants at the time, they often traveled separately.

"Where is she? What do you mean she's not here her tits are here!" The director would grumble. "Ah fuck it, start without her."

I was editing one day and the producer came in skulking around my desk, staring at me.

"Jerry, what do you want?" I would ask.

"Just wanna know,.. where did you get your boob job done?" He would ask, drooling and grabbing his dick.

As I was a full-figured girl, my answer was always "Burger King."

And so on.

I also feel I single handedly brought back the barter system to Los Angeles. Often I would keep a small box of tapes (this was the time of the VHS) in my car for friends. I had a Ford Aerostar van that was heading for the last roundup but I didn't have the heart to put it down. It was due for a smog test and it simply was not passing.

As I sat in the dingy waiting room that smelled of old exhaust and was littered with People magazines from the 70's, I would peek through the window and look at the haggard well-meaning older Hispanic mechanic just shaking his head.

Finally, I got up and walked into the shop.

"So, it's not passing the smog?" I asked, all but twirling a handkerchief in my hand and biting my lip, making my eyes as huge and lost as possible.

He kept telling me in broken English: "It no pass." He would repeat these words while waving his hands over the paperwork. Maybe he was trying to magically make it work or trying to tell me I needed to shoot it.

I looked around the garage and saw about 4 younger guys working on cars. They were taking a mild interest in a female in their midst. With a flourish, I opened the back of the van and feigned surprise.

"Well, no wonder it's not passing. This needs to be taken out." I said in the vein of Scarlet O'Hara and looked at the men now circling the box like vultures. "If this is out of the back and taken away, would it help?" I batted my eyes. The cardboard box had about 20 tapes in it in their clamshell, all color, cases. Dozens of over painted porn girls all but batted their eyes from the pictures.

Many nods and smiles and I drove away with a passed smog test twenty minutes later. Gracias.

Once I did change cars, I went with a Ford Escort. By this time, the era of the DVD was making its way and I could carry a lot more product. And, I did.

I needed a brake job and my money was short. Hey, I worked in porn. Only directors and studio heads make money, not the rest of us great unwashed.

Driving into the local service station, the young man with long hair started quoting me a price for pads and installation to a tune that was going to have me eating instant rice for a month. With tears in my eyes, I remembered what was in the trunk. I popped it open and showed the guy the box.

"If these were gone, would the brakes go on cheaper?" I asked. Again, batting the eyes helped. As well as a box of 10 DVDs, all color and full of pretty naked pictures. He drooled, literally.

Without a word, I was charged for the pads, no labor, and drive home within a half hour. Stopped at In And Out to celebrate. Hey, I had extra money!

Of course, once porn was free on the internet, I ate a lot of that instant rice when I needed a new fan belt. Actually now I have a bike. Ten speed. Tires need air. Damn it.

My first time on a porn set also happened when I was with Porn-Town. Frank wanted to make sure I saw all aspects of the business and he sent me to a set to pick up a box of tapes and get the latest feature started. Things were still being recorded on 30-minute beta tapes at the time.

I had to drive up many steep hills with winding turns deep in the Valley. Yes, that is a pun. Making my way to the once lavish house, I could hear the beginning then middle of a sex scene. The place was trapped in the late 70's and looked it. Smelled like it too. Musty and moldy. Old yellow and orange shag carpet and paneled walls. The moans were loud and sounded like people were being murdered. Through the windows I saw the boom operator, the cameraman, bright blinding lights, a director, and assorted crew people. I waited outside patiently until I heard the director yell 'tape change!' which means they had filled a thirty minute tape and the actors had to pause.

I slipped inside, introduced myself and then saw a few people I had met at the office. Two of them being the performers. I was waiting for the tape to be labeled when they both looked at me from the bed and smiled.

"Hey you, finally got out of your cage huh?" The naked male performer smiled, kneeling in front of the naked female performer, body rocking slowly as sweat poured down his face and chest.

"You staying for lunch?" Said the female on her back, legs akimbo. "I just hope it's not chili again." She said with a pout of her injected lips.

Now, you might think this was hot or something but I assure you, it is the farthest thing from it. Besides this musty and moldy room I was catching the wafting scent of sweaty man balls and other parts of both of them with fluids. The air was thick with it and it was making me queasy. I glanced at the windows and saw they were actually fogging over from the heat in the room. I stopped myself from drawing the word 'Help' in the condensation.

I said I had to get back to the office but talked a bit with them about their significant others, parties they had been to, their pets and families. The box was handed to me and I said my goodbyes. As I backed out I realized, they were still connected. The male was still inside the female as we talked about chili and dog groomers.

Welcome to porn. When I saw them again at an adult industry function, I never got the image out of my head, Seeing it on screen is one thing but when you are four feet away from the action, it's just something you don't forget. Nor do you forget that smell.

Now, having a couch or two in one's office means my office was where people hung out. I didn't mind at all. I loved having people around me and showing them the trailers I was doing and the things I was working on. I was very proud of my work and I showed off constantly. Much like a puppy who learns a new trick, I thrived on the praise.

One such visitor I will call Jack. He was an old school performer/director (weren't they all?) with a face like an apple doll but a heart of gold. He was gray and he chain smoked so he would stop mid-sentence, go out to smoke, then come back in and pick up the thread without missing a beat. He would come in with a fifth of tequila and take out burgers and we would talk. Well, he would talk and I would listen. Often I felt myself nodding but not hearing a word as he never took a breath, except for that smoke. He lived across the street (actually, he moved in across the street once he got a directing contract with us) and would stay until all hours like I did and be there in the morning for my first smoke break as I still smoked. No, I rarely smoked with him. I needed that break of silence to get my ears to stop ringing.

Jack would deliver a box of tapes, a feature, with a script and we would sit down, review the tapes, and outline how he wanted the feature to look. Often, the director's 'vision' and what he shot were miles apart. Yet, the directors got all the credit. But, that was the job. My job, and I was damned good at it.

I was still bleary and sipping my morning coffee when Jack came in looking more haggard than usual and sheepish. He was carrying the box and script and handed it over without meeting my eyes. I opened it and found only eight tapes instead of the usual ten; one them broken beyond repair.

He sighed heavily. "My girlfriend and I had a fight and this got thrown against the wall and I can't reshoot anything." He said sadly. He hung his head like a hound dog and waited for me to rap his nose with a newspaper. I stared at the box and the ruined tapes, others from the office heard the story and crowded around muttering in a slight panic.

We looked over what footage we did have and I read the script. It was a parody of a Mel Gibson movie called Forever Young where

Mel is put in a deep freeze for 25 years then wakes up to see the world and the woman he loved all changed. It took some time but I had an idea. I told him to make a fake diary to read from and make it look like he had just found it and was simply reading a story. I would make it look like he was the narrator and stitch a story together.

It didn't work. He had set up the microphone across the room and the couch he was on was in front of a window with the sun blinding behind him. Basically you could neither hear or see him. I was missing an entire sex scene and a half and now had no story.

Out of sheer frustration, I ended up adding a running sub-title dialogue to the movie from the view of the editor. I tried to be funny (and not make it all anger) and to simulate the major missing part I made it look as if the editor had fallen asleep and simply woke up in another part of the feature.

AVN (Adult Video News) gave it four out of five stars and it sold well. Huzzah. This is called 'polishing a turd to a high gloss shine'. Get it?

Overall, I was very happy at PornTown. I felt respected and was learning more and more about the business every day. Frank was an amazing mentor and I worked hard to make him proud of me. This was where I learned how to patch and re-patch multiple machines and learned every trick that the AVID could do. I would spend hours marking the right cables and making all the adjustments so each output ran smoothly. It was the best lesson I ever taught myself.

Then, out of nowhere, Frank was let go. I got a hug, and a kiss on the cheek, and out the door he went. I felt like I'd been stabbed and couldn't breathe. My lifeline had been dropped into the ocean and sent out to sea. Later I found out this was an upper-management decision. They needed to cut costs so the out-of-town owner of the company swooped in and started chopping. I stared after Frank just blinking, waiting for him to walk back in and say, 'April Fool!'. Anything. But he was gone.

I was shattered.

Before I (or anyone else) knew it the new general manager, I will call him Shifty, was sitting behind Frank's desk. He was a real porn guy: he looked like he sold expired Girl Scout cookies out of the trunk of his car and his side job would have been local pimp. He had dyed black hair and a greasy mustache and just oozed. Period. He oozed.

Frank's well-appointed office was soon crammed with towers of uneven stacks of papers and boating paraphernalia; monkey fist knots as paperweights and gold anchors on the wall. Pictures in frames were of his boat. His wife on the boat. Him on the boat. His dog on the boat. I never knew the name of the damned boat.

He started to staff the place with his people and insisted I needed an assistant. Yes, I was still ignorant at this point. My life line to sanity was gone and I was in the dingy behind the damned boat. I interviewed several people and I picked one out. However, we hired who Shifty wanted instead. He was Shifty's twin with lighter hair. The kind of guy who would have a permanent parking space at the strip club near the airport just for the all-you-can-eat shrimp buf-fet. He said he was down on his luck and was living in a trailer, divorced from his wife and rarely saw his kid. It was a great sob story. I bought it all hook line and sinker. I taught him the ins and outs of the AVID, he knew the basics but I taught him a lot more. He didn't suck and we worked well together. He was my assistant. He edited together compilations and cleaned up the sex scenes I cut. We still worked a lot of hours but in the beginning we were an okay team.

Shifty threw a great deal of money into a new movie with all the PornTown stars called 'Model'. It was a movie about murder and intrigue in the world of modeling. The script was smart and the cast was stunning. With Frank gone, I felt the need to prove myself. I was told by Shifty that we needed to get through this movie and make it great then we would all move forward as one. I believed him.

I put everything I had into the movie. I didn't let Shifty Jr. near this one. 'Model' was all me and was going to stay that way. I added all the special effects and fancy cutting I could muster. I even did a music video that looked like it came straight off MTV. It was the three female leads in the back of a convertible driving down Sunset Blvd. I made many of the shots black and white and used a Rolling Stones song. It was impressive and we used it for the teaser trailer.

I was pushing the new AVID system to its limits and often hitting one effect would un-render an entire segment of video. That being said, every un-render meant a possible hour or more of re-rendering.

I was glad my office had couches because I slept there many a weekend to make sure I had the cut on time with all the effects for the higher-ups. My partner brought me food several times. Jack came over and took care of me too. I was exhausted but I was on fire. I was SO proud of this movie! I've actually looked at it recently and I remember every cut, every frame. I am still very proud of it. I had to create Access Hollywood-type media elements to go with the modeling segments. I had the AVID doing things it wasn't supposed to but it worked! Now, to be clear, this is porn, so the audience around the rather cheesy catwalk was made up of bored grips, over-it lighting people, and the makeup and hair person. It was kind of sad. I had to make it into something.

After sleeping at the office for weeks and slaving over the film, it was ready to show the managers. Shifty, the owner, and the art guy, filed into my room and stood expectantly as I explained what I had done. I showed them the trailer, holding my breath as I hit 'play' and glancing at them as they stared at the screen. The music filled the room and I watched my weeks of effort play across the large computer screen. I knew every cut, every beat, I was very proud of my work.

It was a triumph! They all shook hands and patted each other on the back with wide smiles. Then they left. They left. Without one word to me. They simply walked out. I stared at my opened door as the air was sucked out of the room. I could hear them congratulating themselves all the way to Shifty's office. The office to his door closed and all was silent.

It was the first time porn had kicked me in the teeth and it would not be the last.

A few days later and still with no praise or acknowledgment, just a deadline, I sat in that huge office and grumbled to myself. I heard Shifty on the phone saying how great it was and I watched the mock ups of the box cover roll by. Sadly, for the great movie I had made, they made a typical porn cover. Half-naked chicks with the title in this horrible first-year graphic student font.

Next to me was a stack of AVN Magazines. I looked over the glossy covers and picked one off the top. At this time the magazine was thick and I often looked for ads for movies I had done in the pages. I had to make a choice; do I stay in porn and put up with this kind of treatment or was this a one-time thing? Do I go back out in to mainstream post production and work 18-hour days 6 days a week? PornTown and porn was basically a 9 to 5 with creative freedom.

I opened the magazine and saw an ad for a movie I had finished the month before. I knew the shots of the feature, the music I had used and I could hear it. Then I kept flipping. The largest advertising section was the center and it was bursting with ads from a place I will call Supreme Movies. At that time, Supreme was the biggest and most prestigious company in adult. They had brought back the studio system of the old days and would sign girls like old film stars. Everyone wanted to be a Supreme Babe. Their biggest director was, I will call him, Sam Johnson. I had made a point of watching his films because I admired the approach he took to filmmaking in general. Porn or not, I studied the greats like any film student.

It was then and there I made my choice: If I was going to be an editor in this business, I was going to be best. I was going to work for Supreme and I was going to edit for Sam and I was going to win an AVN Award. I closed the magazine and went home for the day.

In honor of my new found career path, I treated myself like any woman would and did something to my hair. I went from blonde to a strawberry red and I liked it very much. I bounced into work the next day, all smiles and excitement. I punched in the security code to my office and it beeped red. I blinked and did it again, and a third time.

Shifty came out of his office and smiled like a shark eyeing a blood red steak.

"Could I see you for a moment?" He said and beckoned me into his/Frank's old office. I stepped into the 'dick wagging' decor of pictures of his boat (did I mention he had a boat?) and sat. I swore the chair was sticky. It felt humid in the large space. Well, it used to be a large space, but now it was filled up with non-earned bravado and boat pictures.

"What's up?" I asked, still pretty oblivious to what was coming.

"Well, 'Model' is done and we are moving in a different direction so we are letting you go." He said. Just like that. He cut the lifeline to the dingy I was in and I was about to float out to sea.

Of course, I had that 'bucket of cold water thrown on me' feeling and I am sure I went white. He had made me so many promises of long-term employment and being part of the team. Many hours were spent in his office reassuring me that I was a vital part of this team. Promises of a long future were doused in lighter fluid and Shifty had the match. It was then I realized he had been bringing his own people in slowly and getting rid of anyone Frank had ever hired. This included warehouse and even accounting staff. He offered my assistant, Shifty Jr., my job and he took it. Down the road, Shifty Jr. would tell people he taught me everything I knew. And, Shifty Jr. became a director.

"So, you lied to me," I said. It wasn't a question.

"Yep." He said with a smile. He sat back in his chair, hands folded over his beer belly, very proud of himself.

How could I argue with blatant shithead honesty? It happened one year to the day I started.

I was paid a severance and was out the door. Side note: I only ever dyed my hair red one more time in my life and got fired the next day as well. I've never done it again.

But, my goal was clear. I set out to find another editing job in adult. That landed me at a landmark.

WorkHorse Porn.

CHAPTER FOUR

If you have spent any time working in adult, you've worked at WorkHorse. It's a thing. Everyone has been through those offices and they have been around forever. I honestly don't remember how I got the job there but I am sure it was through someone I knew at PornTown beforehand. The place may as well have had a revolving door with a waiting room. Now serving, #5438 for a sales position! Now serving #5439, stockroom position! Now serving #5440, Editing! That's me! Right this way.

WorkHorse was about as ghetto as it gets. It was what a porn company was at the time; run down and piecemeal. Shabby carpet and thin plaster walls served as offices. That office space was carved out of the warehouse space. Every porn company has that template of offices patched onto warehouse space. The offices are really an afterthought and if they were not peddling porn, they could be selling auto parts. I know I've used the auto parts analogy before but that's exactly what it is like. Paperwork was strewn everywhere, the scent of gasoline and grease, and nudie calendars pinned to the walls. The edit bay, as it were, was a real treat.

This place was very behind the times. I didn't do any actual editing. Everything was making compilations (i.e.: movies made up of scenes from other movies) or cut-downs (i.e.: making a movie shorter to fit a certain length). Basically like a recycling center. Taking old worn-out porn and shining it up, repackaging it, and making another tired dime on old scenes. That practice has yet to stop and never will.

When most mainstream actors sign a contract, they get residuals for every time that movie gets shown anywhere. In porn, a girl or guy does a scene, gets paid and bye-bye baby. The producers own that image forever. Yes, forever. They will repackage and fold, spindle, and mutilate that scene to make as much profit as possible in perpetuity. They can take all the scenes with blondes, you got a new comp. All brunettes, comp. Big boobs, MILFS, tattooed, anything! Companies, once a movie is finished, add tags to every scene and put them in a spreadsheet. When they needed a new release, they just run the numbers, slap the scenes together with a sparkly new opening (that took about ten minutes to create and looked it), and poof! New release!

I spent most of my time at WorkHorse making hour and half movies into fifty minute movies. They could be sold to any outlet with that run time, domestic or foreign. I got the spread sheet with the tapes weekly. It was a lot of tapes and a lot of machines in very loud, unbuffered rooms. There were two edit bays, one across from the other, with a hallway leading to the warehouse in between where they repaired axles and did tire rotation. I mean… packed boxes of porn. The edit bay was the final afterthought of the place. The tape machines were at an angle in this wooden contraption that held the computer and keyboard. It was really strange.

I remember getting a bunch of movies and one was by Ed Wood of Plan 9 From Outer Space fame. Seems he slipped into porn at the end of his illustrious career. The film was a story about three people in an apartment complex hanging out by the pool. It was two white girls and one black man. It was shot sometime in the early 70's. I remember the colors being painfully bright. One orange bikini gave me that 'someone just took my picture with a flash and I can still see the pop of light when I look away' thing. They had some polite conversation and were soon, all three, in bed having sex. One problem.

Mr. Wood never picked up any sound equipment. The entire movie was music. Oh, and subtitles. Over the sex. Yes, it was a lot of 'oohs' and 'ahhs' and 'oh baby' typed on the screen.

I will say, it was lit well and in focus. Can not fault him for that.

There were a lot of old 70's movies in the WorkHorse catalog that were only vaguely about sex but we had to use them anyway. Lots of hair in these movies. Everywhere. Lots.

I have added this company into this book for one reason. I became friends with one of the sales team, Ray Peters. He factors in this story later, which is why I wanted to mention this little stopover in my career. He had been in the industry for a while and was aiming higher than this place. Then again, everyone that worked there was aiming out the door ASAP. He was a nice guy with a wife and kids and I liked him. He even had me and my little family over for dinner once. He made us feel very at home.

Now, this is normal. People being nice and becoming friends. He was an average build kind of guy with a nice smile. Down the road, I don't know what happened, but he became obsessed with working out and lost some weight. A lot of weight. A strong wind would have toppled him. This was after his divorce. When I saw him at conventions later, he had this wild look in his eyes and sort of looked around me. I follow his Facebook, he still works out a lot. Porn is not for normal people. Or, you can go into porn normal and come out different.

I remember being called into the supervisor's office a few times and I truly do not remember why. The boss was the owner's nephew. The place was run by an Armenian family and lots of relatives were running around the place.

More than likely, I was spending more time out of my edit bay then in. But, the kind of work we had to do was literally push a button and sit for an hour. It was like watching bad hairy paint dry. Movies from the 70's, remember? Lots of hair.

I don't remember lasting there long. But I went from there to what I thought was a step up as I would be actually editing on a non-linear system, an AVID as I had learned!

It wasn't better.

CHAPTER FIVE

Miriam and David were an older brother and sister team that ran Bright Sky Films. Also Armenians. More family. Scary building. It was another place with offices crammed around a warehouse down some street that looked abandoned. There was bar tucked into the next block over. I never went there.

They had an AVID and I was to be the head editor paid by the feature. As I finish a movie, I would get a check. I was freelance with a time clock and my own edit suite. Once I was done with a movie, it went to the music guy. He was WAY into soundtracks and turned me on to some very cool music. He didn't stay long. He was, honestly, too talented to be there. Then again, we all were.

Bright Sky, like WorkHorse, is what I call a Transition Company. It was the kind of place that you changed the name of on your resume and dropped as soon as you could. It was where you made industry connections and cashed a paycheck to get to the next, much better, job.

The building was two floors and looked more like a large cinder block. No name on the door, obviously. The lobby had the kind of black velvety porn furniture you would expect along with the brass and glass tables. AVN Magazines (old ones) fanned out on the table like a doctor's office. It was tacky. There was no receptionist but there was a reception desk with a phone that wasn't plugged in. I worked on the second floor with the sales team. One of my first directors was Hawaii Joe.

He was a performer that also directed and he often asked me to be in his films. He was not very tall, with dark hair, dark eyes, and the sweetest smile. His voice was soft and he called me 'honey' a lot. It wasn't a bad thing, just meant he liked me. He calls me 'honey' to this day. It only made me nuts a few times when we would be talking about an edit and he would lift a hand and say 'But, honeyhoneyhoney, listen." It was never ever in a mean way. He just needed to get his thoughts straight. He was never gross about asking me to be in his films or touched me the wrong way. He was a businessman but also a gentleman. We still stay in touch and he is retired now, happily watching his grandchildren grow up. He was the first director to trust my work and rarely made any changes. He knew I knew what I was doing. In the future, before he retired, he asked me to do some work for him and I met him at a coffee shop in Hollywood. The parking was hell and the drive into town was worse. But this was Joe. I would do a lot for a director that treated me like a person.

The next director I worked with was Francois Clousot. A tall, dark, and handsome French man with a deep voice and a heavy French accent. He looked and sounded like something out of an old movie. I expected him to have on a beret, smoking a cigarette, with a baguette under his arm. He liked to sit with me as I worked so we became a team. I was never sure about working with someone but working with him I learned a lot. I learned why he held certain shots and why he ditched others. He also knew this was porn. There was artistry and then there was 'we can't see his dick.'

When we got tired or needed a break, I would put on some music so we could unwind. Often, it was Barbie Girl by Aqua. No idea why, it just cracked us up and I would play it loud! Hearing him say the opening words with that French accent was a scream!

One day, during one of our breaks, I finally had to call him out on something.

"Dude, I am sorry but with that dark hair in a faux pompadour and that accent… You remind me of Pepe Le Pew!" I said with a small laugh, praying he wasn't going to be offended and would get the joke because, seriously, he DID remind me of the cartoon skunk. He still does! Either he would get it or smack me over the head with that baguette.

He was wearing a black leather vest over a t-shirt that day. He stood slowly and tugged at the vest to smooth out the fabric. He looked stern and I thought I was dead.

"Madam! I am ze-insulted!" He said with an exaggerated accent.

He pulled open the snaps of the vest and on the t-shirt was the face of Pepe Le Pew! The drawing took up the entire shirt! I lost it and he laughed. Seems his sister worked at a major studio and he had a hefty Le Pew collection! I later saw the collection. Mugs, frames, clothes, statues.... everything Le Pew! We laughed and put on Barbie Girl one more time.

The owners of Blue Sky liked to think we were all a family. They often asked how I was doing, how was my life, etc. Except, when it came to money.

Miriam would be all smiles and calling me 'Dahhling' in her heavy Armenian accent over the morning coffee. Later in the day I would bring her a tape with a completed movie on it and stand patiently, waiting for my check. She would open the case and look at the tape like I had handed her a watch to be appraised.

"How I know this not blank, hm? How I know you not rip me off?" She said with no humor. She was serious.

"I can play it for you upstairs in the deck." I offered, trying to appease.

"No, you steal from me. Everyone steal from me." She would say, berating me as she begrudgingly wrote out my check. This happened every time. Every friggin' time. I was doing two to three movies a week.

David had another way of handling his employees. With the new AVID there was simply a lot of rendering to be done. Basically, setting the machine to do a task and walking away for hours. Yes, you could check in and monitor it but mainly it just needed to be left alone to work. Around this time, they were discovering the internet and DVD authoring. He had hired these two kids (guys) to do the DVD stuff and they also would hit a button and have to wait. The three of us sometimes worked late into the night, which is pretty common for post-production.

However, David did not trust us.

He would lock the doors and gates when he left at 5 pm. If we wanted to be let out of the cage, we had to call him. He would show up in his shorts and flip-flops, grumbling.

"Why you here so late? What work you do? Prove to me! You rip me off! You steal!" Often this was 10 pm or later. We would offer to show him but he would just wave his hands, watch us like a hawk as we went to our cars. I am shocked he didn't search us like a department store detective. I am sure he was scanning our bags for any outline of a rogue DVD. Sure! We just had to have copies of Milf Herder #48 to give to our friends. Personally, I used it as a coaster. He would relock the doors and take off.

When I say doors, I mean the glass doors and the heavy metal gates that he latched with a chain and padlock. He said he was doing it for our protection. But, he was sure we were stealing and this way we couldn't leave with his product. If we wanted to get food, we had to do it before he locked the doors. If there was a fire… we were screwed. We ordered pizza a lot because it was the only thing that could be slid under the gate.

Gonzo porn was invented at Blue Sky. You can say anything you want but I was a witness.

When a new director wanted to work with the company, David would send them upstairs to the edit bay and I was to look at their footage and give them my opinion.

Often I sent them back down with a smile but told David no. It was his dime, but the footage would be beyond amateur and there was no money to be made. Often the footage was out of focus or the audio was all static. Usually, this was a guy with his girlfriend or a guy who convinced a girl to get into porn. Bad casting couch stuff.

Then J Bone walked into my life.

He was a tall ginger with thick black rim glasses and tattooed muscled arms. He was warm and friendly and I liked him right away. He was a film student and as he grew as a pornographer, he never stopped learning about the process of filmmaking. He handed over the camera and tapes and I started to watch.

The set up was simple. Two guys, walking along, find a camera in an alley. They turn it on and start filming everything they see. They go home and one of the guy's girlfriend shows up. She asks about the camera and then starts a strip tease. This leads to a sex scene.

It was brilliant. It was simple. Also, it was shot well; clear and in focus, and well-lit.

I watched more and my mouth hung open. It was elegant in its simplicity. I looked at J Bone and said. "Run. Get out of here. You belong at Supreme."

His eyes got wide. "I can't get anyone to talk to me there!" Supreme, at that time, was the Gold Standard and anyone who was anyone worked there.

I pulled out my book of numbers and dialed Ray Peters. This was the sales guy I met at WorkHorse and now he was working at Supreme. I told him J's story and said I was sending him over. Ray said he couldn't wait and we hung up.

J's eyes were wide. "You are awesome." He said with a bright smile.

This is what I did for people. I got people together that needed to be together. I did that a lot. To this day when I hear someone needs help, my brain goes to 'who do I know that could help'.

I did edit a few things for J at Bright Sky but he went to Supreme fairly quickly. It was because of him, I got hired there. But, I am getting ahead of myself.

The last straw for me at Bright Sky was a gay director who was pulling a fast one but decided not to tell me. He was contracted to turn in a five scene movie twice a month. He was tall and slender with bright bleached blond hair. We would sit and go over the footage and he would tell me the order of the scenes.

After a few months, he began reusing scenes. Only one per movie.

"Miriam and David know. They said it was okay." He told me, casually, like I should just know this.

I was still pretty naive and just nodded and went with it. I didn't know the whole ins and outs of the business yet. In the future, I would learn this was common practice. Re-using scenes, that is. Well, stealing from the bosses (stealing from The Man) was common too. Cause the Man kept trying to keep you down and take all your money! They gave you money to shoot a movie they approved then gave you contracts to keep doing just that and they keep paying you. Lying dogs.

I did it for two months then one day David and Miriam burst into the edit bay screaming in their language; their faces beet red. It sounded like two loud and large crows flapping and swooping in on the same target.

"You steal from us! You and the fag! You steal from us!" David yelled as Miriam started to tear apart my desk looking for my hidden stash of riches. Power cords took the air. Cases with tapes inside were pulled open and flung around the room. I think even my purse was overturned. They were sad when they only found my car keys and a tin of Altoids.

"You steal! He pay you to lie and steal!" She screamed. Seems the director did NOT tell Miriam and David. He was getting paid for five scenes yet only shooting four, therefore, pocketing the extra cash. He didn't share any of it with me. The information or the money!

They fired me on the spot. Right after I quit.

I gathered my things in a box, said goodbye to people, and headed out. While in the lobby, Miriam cried and David held his arms out.

"Why you go?" David said and hugged me tight. His little stocky body sweating.

"We treat you like daughter and now you go!" Miriam cried from the velvet couch and then got up to hug me.

I had never been more confused in my life.

I think my tires left skid marks in the street as I left.

CHAPTER SIX

When J Bone got hired at Supreme, he wasted no time in making sure I worked there. Yes, I had my own credentials, but he always credits 'an editor' with helping his start in porn. He never mentions me by name, never has. Here, I will return the favor and credit his influence that got me into Supreme. J Bone helped me get the job at Supreme. But you will not get his real name, favor returned.

This is where I became Sonny Malone.

With this upward trajectory in my career, I deserved a new, official, porn name. My nickname in real life is Sonny so that was easy. The last name I got from Showgirls. Nomi Malone. My current favorite bad movie at the time. It sounded like the name a gangster would use. I loved it.

Of course, Google it now and you will see it is also the name of the main character in the 80's cult classic Xanadu. A high school favorite of mine. I did not put two and two together there until many years later. In the 80's, I thought Michael Beck was hot and I roller-skated with ribbons in my hair. I have no shame.

I remember the day I got the job. I did this little dance around my apartment like I had finally grabbed the brass ring. I replaced the words to 'I Got Rhythm" to "I Got Supreme". They had the Supreme Babes. They had the best directors. The best of everything. Now, they had me.

At this time, the Supreme offices were a converted warehouse in Van Nuys. No shock there. The offices attached to the warehouse here were slightly better. The walls of the edit bays were carpeted in an attempt to look like mainstream audio buffering. Surprised I didn't see empty egg cartons up there. The driveway was a pain in the ass. The spaces were angled so you could park as you pulled in but they had blocked the exit with more warehouse space so you had to back out. It was insane and completely impractical. When I finally saw this Jewel of the Porn crown I realized something. This place was a good example of a company 'playing at being legit'. Legally, everything was very above board. However, the facility was run down and cheap. Just like most of the equipment. The bloom was coming off the rose quickly.

Originally, there was a punch card time clock system. Some people took advantage of that and soon after I got there, there was a hand scan system to keep everyone honest. I still never understand why people feel the need to 'get away' with things.

"Man, this place sucks." A deep voice pouts.

"Oh yea, it's terrible! They pay us a decent wage and give us holidays and vacations. We even got medical insurance! Sucks man! How dare they!" I always wanted to say. Eventually, I did. I mean the place wasn't paradise but we kept the jobs, right? If you hate it that much, do me the favor and quit. I did! But more of that later!

My first boss was Dickey. Now, if you are a grown man nearing 40 named Richard, but you were under 5 foot 8 inches with a buzz cut, who always wore long jean shorts and tan Doc Martens, would you opt for the name Dickey?

When he walked through the place, he had this kinetic energy and bright fake smile and was sure he was one of the guys but he was management, everyone knew better. He had the kind of walk where his head led him and he charged forward through the halls always on a mission. Always in a hurry.

Sadly, no one respected him. He simply brought down any heat that came from above so he was just a conduit for upper management. He would stomp around the place trying to be one of the guys and be cool. He even drank with the guys (when he was the one who bought the beer, they never invited him when it was on their dime) but he was never truly accepted. I understood him. I was never included in anything with the guys because I wasn't a guy. I was the only female in post-production and even after I left, that never changed. It was as simple as that. I befriended Dickey. And, I remember the day he was fired.

It was just a management trimming thing, I thought. Then I realized who was going to take over and it was Roberto. Roberto had been Dickey's best buddy and looked like he belonged in the lineup of Metallica. Tall, deep voice, long hair metal looking dude. He was Dickey's right hand (and with the same long shorts and Doc Martens) and eventually, when that hand was cut, it was Roberto who took over the job happily. He had been a drinking buddy with the guys too but he was respected since he often bought the beer. I lost touch with Dickey. It had been a site-specific relationship

My original schedule was a 4 - 10 system. I worked for four days, ten hours each. My days off were Tuesday, Wednesday, and Thursday. I worked over the weekends from 6 am to 4 pm. I loved it! Went to the beaches and museums weekly because I could go on the days when most people were at work!

I had my own little office decorated with Disney posters. I had them up to counteract the amount of porn I was seeing. I didn't realize until later that that was why I had put them up. I would tape Saturday Night Live from the night before and let the tape run until it ran out. My co-worker, Derek, and I would watch the show over breakfast. After SNL, we found a show with Lorenzo Lamas called The Immortal. It was an amazingly bad Highlander rip off and we eagerly watched all 22 episodes!

If we got tired during the shift, we would bounce a tennis ball to each other up and down the long hallways. When this Rock A Billy kid, Gerry, joined the team (I mean seriously, he had a teal 50's looking car, the greaser pompadour and leather jacket) we would have tag races through the halls. My favorite was the audio guy, Norman. I lost count of the times I would walk into the audio bay and he would have his feet up, snoring. I made a point of going into his bay a half hour before the management came in, bringing him coffee, and making sure he was awake and functional. When Norman did leave, we did stay in touch. He even moved to another state and we remained friends for a long time. He has always made me smile.

Of course, working with young fit guys, we ordered a lot of junk food. The amount of weight I put on was criminal! Sadly, we went to the 9-5, five days a week within six months of my being hired.

The actual work was fun! I worked with many directors and learned a lot of things about the AVID I didn't know. Especially when we had a mainstream technician service the machines. I stayed glued to them and asked a ton of questions. It also gave me several contacts in the industry that I would find useful later.

My goal was to edit for Sam Johnson, known around the office as SJ. SJ's favorite editor, Connor, was going to be leaving the company to move to mainstream. As I felt I was the next best editor there, and many directors loved my work, I was hopeful that SJ would work with me next. SJ was the goal, after all. Connor sat me down and showed me the way SJ liked things to be edited. He showed me some tricks and walked me through the process. I studied with him for weeks and was always there when SJ showed up. I made sure to make friends.

Then, George Clooney showed up. Okay, his name was Damon but he was very handsome and looked like he walked off an ad for premium whiskey. SJ of course gravitated towards him, as we all did, and I was passed over. Damon had come from mainstream and was going through a tough time personally. Porn was a place for him to settle (his personal rock bottom) and lick his wounds as he healed. We spent many hours in his bay going over edits and that would lead to lunch which would lead to talking about our problems. I was glad he felt he could talk to me and I could talk to him. He was another one I stayed in touch with when he left the company. He went back to mainstream and has done very well for himself in reality television.

While George/Damon worked his magic over the entire company, including the owner, I remained with my other directors. SJ was still out of reach. One was Felix Jaymes. I truly liked him. He had a bright smile and a warm personality. His humor matched mine and we always had fun working together. He was a bleeding heart that poured his pain into every film. We did one autobiographical feature called Lovely Lady. It was about a guy (Felix) who had fallen for a porn star and of course, she broke his heart. For our screener, we used real music, music that was meant for the scenes he had written. Songs from Siouxie and Banshees and The Cure. It was beautiful and painful and perfect. Of course, we had to change it all for the release, but for us, the original lived on. He won Best Director and Best Screenplay for that one. It was a deeply personal film for him.

After that feature, he changed. Physically and emotionally. I can't say exactly what was going on with him. All I saw was him becoming very thin and gaunt and he covered his bony arms with tribal work black tattoos. The light from his eyes had faded and his humor was gone.

He was sitting in my edit bay, grumbling over a script, very unhappy about some changes he was told to make. Normally he would be leaning on my desk and we'd be talking about anything and everything yet this time he was all but cowering in the corner, hunched in the chair, staying in the dark like a vampire avoiding sunlight. I half expected him to hiss at me. This was the time in adult films when you couldn't have too much BDSM in a regular porn feature. And not too much hardcore sex in a BDSM feature. It was truly bullshit backward and it was making us both nuts.

I was editing out a scene and he lost it.

"What are you doing?!" He said, his voice raised as he flew at me from the dark corner. I looked for a cape and a pair of fangs.

I jumped a little and looked at the notes I had been given that matched his.

"We have to take that part out. But I can - "

"Damn it! NO!" He screamed and hurled his copy of the script across the small room. It bounced off the side of my head, hit the wall, then hit the floor.

I was stunned as I watched him turn into a bat and fly out. Several of the other editors came in to see if I was okay. I should have been crying or upset. I was just stunned. And checking my neck for puncture wounds.

The next thing I knew, I was in Dickey's office with Felix. Felix looked shaky and wide-eyed as he apologized. I, of course, said it was no problem and that I understood even though I didn't. He was crackling with nerves and I wanted to hug him as I had a hundred times before. But I couldn't get close. It broke my heart.

I never saw Felix again and I finished the movie without him.

He ended up directing elsewhere.

This was where my rose-colored glasses began to crack more.

The day shift of post-production was myself and about 7 to 8 other guys. We were told to take our daily allotted ten-minute break together. At the same time. Every day. I was still smoking at the time so I took the time to do just that out in the weird angled driveway. You couldn't go too far because the breaks were short and we were in the middle of an industrial park. No 7-11 in sight. We would all visit and talk and shake off the work day.

While standing in the driveway, we watched a brand new yellow two-door Mercedes convertible, with dealer plates, drive in and go all the way to the owner's office door. We wondered if an adult actress was going to get out then wondered who was going to turn the car around for her in our fucked up driveway. Then, another car pulled in. Mercedes. Different color. Different roof. Same kind of plates. Then another. And another until the entire driveway was full with two-door brand new Mercedes. Five in all. We all sort of blinked and watched the drivers get out and make their way to the front office. I lit another cigarette and watched the owner of Supreme and his business partner begin to shop.

They were too busy to go to the dealership. They had to wave their dicks for all of us to see. Meanwhile, I had just had a conversation with another employee who had been turned down for a raise and I knew he was on ramen for the week for his lunches. A few of the guys were supporting their families and struggling to make ends meet and these assholes were picking out new cars. It was such a blatant display of flaunting their wealth, it made me sick. It was all I could do to stop myself from grabbing a flag and start chanting "Vive La Revolution' and get the guys behind me on board with a musical number from Les Miz.

Dickey quickly came out of post and hustled us all back in even though our break was not over. We all crushed out our barely smoked cigarettes (counting those pennies gone) and heard the door close behind us. The rest of our break was spent crammed in the hallway then taking turns to clock back in. We all sat at our very old equipment and tried to go back to work. It killed morale in the department for weeks. We were limping on old equipment and being berated to get the job done no matter what. However, Mercedes had to be bought.

This was where my paycheck bounced. All of your checks bounced. But, the owners had new cars that showed up every day so that was good right? It had been a bank error as the company moved money to a different account. Still, it got to the point that when we got paid, we all caravanned to the bank where the checks were drawn on to get real cash. The tellers knew us and it was some kind of right of passage to see who would get there first. They eventually arranged direct deposit for us. We all still went to the bank to make sure the money was really there.

The owner's Mercedes was yellow. His business partner, baby blue.

This was also my first official FBI lecture. At the time, there was this do's and don't's list of things you could and could not show in 'normal' porn. It was called The Law of Laws List since it was a lawyer who drafted it. It was basically a list of things that had had legal action taken against it in states around the country. These were acts that had been under prosecution in other states and the porn company lost. We kept these things out of the movies so we would not have to make multiple copies for domestic distribution. Oh, and so we wouldn't be sued. That too.

These things were ridiculous. Like, no penetrating a female with anything that was not phallus-like. Such as no cucumbers. No veggies? Why am I here? Yea, you get the picture. In this 'anything goes world' now, this just seems so silly.

You can find the list online. Having just re-read it, it reads now like things you HAVE to have in your movie or don't bother. Then, there was to be no male/male or trans penetration. No Bi-sexual movies either. No interracial (black woman/white man). No incest topics! Some companies would go out of business now with their 'stepmother/step-rest of the family' series! The buffet had been closed! It was vanilla sex or nothing! This was 2001 when Bush decided to try a crackdown on the adult industry. You see how well that worked, right? Except for one I never understood. No coffins. I so do not want to know why that one was even there.

Anyway, we were told that if the police raided the place, just put our hands up and let the officers take us. The owner would have you bailed out of jail before dawn.

No, we were never raided. I knew if we were, he would just leave us there and hire replacements for all of us at a lower salary. His car wouldn't fit all of us anyway. It was only a two-seater!

My first AVN Nomination, I did not win. Supreme didn't give me AVN Award Show Tickets. I had to call AVN myself, say who I was and I asked how much tickets would be for a nominated person. I was given tickets free and I have not paid for one since! But I was so excited about being nominated that I drank way too much and actually wept a few tears when I didn't win. The person I was sitting with was a gay director who just rolled their eyes at me and berated me to get over it. I didn't make a big scene but I did start drinking water pretty fast and tune out Mr. Wonderful who kept huffing at me and telling me I was being stupid. We were at one of the large round tables in the Sands hotel event space before they went 'legit' at the Hard Rock with real theater seating (that no one sits in). The buffet at the back of the room was overflowing with shrimp and porn stars. I had made the rounds and said hello to the people I had seen at the office; performers and directors, then I sat to lick my wounds and suffer my loss.

At this point, by the door, lights and cameras were following a guy with long blond hair and a busty blond at his side. I looked up, like everyone did, and saw Vince Neil. At this point, I was feeling drunk and very low. He made his way through the crowd and spotted two seats at our table, noticed me, smiled, and made his way over.

"I know you!" He smiled. "From Sunset Strip!" He said with a big smile. My partner was a tattoo artist at Sunset and we had met the entire band, Motley Crue, several times. I was slightly shocked he remembered me. He hugged me tight and introduced his girl. She was very sweet.

"You okay?" He asked.

"Oh, I'm good. Was up for an award but I didn't win." I shrugged with a small smile.

"Oh hell girl, whatcha drinkin'?" He said and bought me drinks for the rest of the night. The gay director tried to be pals but Vince's attention was on me. When anyone came over to take his picture, he made sure he had an arm around his girl and the other arm around me. He made my pity party of a night very special.

Once I had that nomination, SJ noticed me. Also, Damon was looking to move on. He had been through enough in his life and wanted to get going to something else as soon as he could. I will confess to just a little worship of Damon and his talents but I was also his friend. I mean, he was extremely hot and he was MY friend.

He had gotten a new apartment and wanted to buy a few things to decorate it so he asked me to go shopping with him.

He took us out to lunch at the local mall and we wandered into Pier One. We moved to the large rugs at the back wall. At that point, I noticed a pretty brunette girl checking out Damon so hard I thought she was going to bang him on the back of the head and drag him off to her cave.

Damon was oblivious so I decided to have some fun. See, I mentioned, I'm a bigger girl so obviously (as this girl glared at me with daggers) not his type. He and I were friends and that was it.

I caught her eye and gently touched Damon's arm.

"Hey, how about this for the living room?" I asked as I stroked the fabric of a large area rug. "Nice and neutral for the furniture," I added and glanced at the girl to make sure she wasn't picking up a lamp to hurl at me.

"Yea, I like it. Did you see these end tables?" He asked and led me to the furnishings. I kept a hold of his arm and he didn't even notice. The girl all but threw fireballs and then turned to leave angrily.

I told Damon all of this later and he just laughed.

"Was she hot?" He asked with a smile.

"No. If she was, I would have introduced you. After she stabbed me, of course."

He respected me, which was something I didn't feel I got a lot of in porn (not since Frank at Porn Town) and I would look for that respect down the road and never find it. He had brought a mainstream aspect to dealing with people to porn and I wished was the norm. I was wrong. He was sort of like the guy in the Dos Exxes beer commercials and way too smooth to be here. Remember, I worshipped. I can say these things.

When he knew how badly I wanted to advance in adult, he was the perfect gentleman and angled SJ towards me. He worked with me like the previous kid had and taught me the things SJ liked. Eventually, I showed Damon what SJ really liked because I had studied it.

When I finally got the chance to edit for the man, I poured all I had into the feature. He would sit with me and we would go over what he liked and didn't and why. I remember shaking a lot and trying to stay calm. I didn't want to blow it.

"Sex needs to have a reason," SJ said. His voice was like cigarette smoke wrapped in velvet. Warm and soft with a lilt and a growling edge. "When I get a script, I like to make sure the sex is part of the story. Not just there for the hell of it. There needs to be some emotion involved." He always used the same writer. Oddly enough, she was a woman. Her scripts were a mix of melodrama and true storytelling about relationships and emotions. I believed the characters were real.

So, when I edited, I made sure to keep that in mind. I would look for possible emotional moments between the actors rather than just 'edit the sex'. Of course, finding those 'emotional' moments was like trying to find a polar bear eating vanilla ice cream in a blizzard, but you see my point.

The first movie I edited for SJ was The Parlor. It starred Jenna Jameson (the current reining Supreme Babe) and her then-husband, Jay. Finding emotion between them was not difficult. The couple had been together off-screen for a while and were truly in love. They were both good actors outside of the sex. It was shot well and SJ and I worked well together! It was to be my first award for editing.

I had done it. I made the goal that I aimed for sitting in my Porn Town office. I was working for Supreme. I was editing for SJ. I won an AVN award for Best Editing. My work was done here. I could leave porn.

Clearly, I didn't.

When the company moved from Van Nuys to Hollywood, things changed. A lot.

The new place was a white stucco building in Hollywood across from a car dealership. The owner was becoming obsessed about being legit in Hollywood so he had the company name slapped on the building in big light-up letters you could see from the freeway.

Porn runs in cycles. Hollywood discovers it and some porn performers might do cross-over work in the mainstream then within ten years, it's driven back to the basements of Van Nuys.

I want to say something about 'crossover' actors. And, let me say again, this is only my opinion. No porn actor ever crosses over. Ever. Oh sure, you can fool yourself that a performer is acting in mainstream. You know when a mainstream actor gets an Oscar and they are forever known as 'Academy Award Winning So-And-So?'. A porn actor will ALWAYS BE 'Adult Performer So-And-So.' You can never ever wash that off. Think of all the adult actors that have crossed to mainstream. All of them. Try not to say their name without adding 'porn star; to it. Go ahead, I dare you. Nope, not even Tracy Lords. You still think of her as that 'girl who did porn'. You know you do. The one who did Entourage. The one who did a movie with Lindsay Lohan. It's a short list. They all come back to Van Nuys. If not physically, mentally, and emotionally.

The owner of Supreme bought the entire brass and glass four-story white stucco building and slowly moved all the current tenants out. Or, they didn't want to be in the same building as a porn company. The front office of Supreme was circular and draped with white sheer panel curtains against walls with no windows. The furniture was white leather and even the bowl of M&Ms was Supreme white. Only white. The floor was white tiles. However, the front desk was a cheap fake wood IKEA pressboard piece and had cables running all over the place and a piece of gray duct tape holding one panel down. It looked tacky as hell.

See what I mean? Playing at being a company. Their booth at AVN looked nicer. Same curtains.

This front office was considered a showpiece, however, employees were not allowed to walk through it. No, I am not kidding. We would get off the elevator and we were allowed to look at the very expensive lobby. Then, we had to take a half-hidden door to the left and go down a long hallway, use the hand stamp just to open the door to enter the office then walk up a flight of stairs, then down the other side to the hallway, near the front door, to clock in. We could see the glass doors to the lobby from the time clock. We just had to make a huge circle to get to it. We were the great unwashed. Not to be seen. I'm surprised we weren't microchipped like pets so they could track our every move. Post-production was on the second floor. There was also a separate set of stairs hidden from the main offices. Going down to the kitchen, we were always spotted. Like the kids you tell to stay in their rooms if the parents were having a cocktail party. If we ever came out when the owner was showing off the swanky first floor, he would steer people into the conference room faster than he planned. I think he thought of us as those feral cats you know you shouldn't feed because we just keep coming back.

Instead of offices, we now had cubicles. This was fine except for the partitions that were used. They were from an old IT company and were of different heights. They still had the stickers on them from the previous company. The place looked cheap right down to the linoleum flooring. Sound at least had a booth so they could work properly. We were all told to wear headphones. Most of us brought our own. Well, we had to. They were not provided.

We had a very small employee kitchen on the first floor. It only had three or four small tables. The owner was all about the latest gadgets for the first floor so when the Keurig coffee machine was a new thing, he got one for the kitchen. Once we all knew it was there, we wanted to try it out! How dare we! Every time the owner saw someone go into the kitchen, he would follow them. Every time.

"Another one?" He would try to joke with a fake smile. The way he would sneak up on us made us all jump when he poked his head into the room. Then he made the rounds to see who had cups on their desks. He rarely came to the second floor but for this, he did.

He then thought we were drinking too much coffee and not doing enough work. It was gone the next day.

After my successful work with SJ, I was given all the new directors to work with. These were people that had been with the company for a while but were moving in a new direction. One was Darwin Rechaud. Soon to be called D. Reck.

He was a photographer that wanted to move into directing, so he was given a shot. His work was fun and easy to edit. He knew what he wanted and he shot it that way. He was often nervous that he would be moved back to being only a photographer and would watch my edits closely but after one movie, had complete confidence in my work. I should say here, every director was nervous regarding the owner's opinion. Each would come to my desk like they just crept into the darkened attic in a horror movie, constantly looking over their shoulder for some imaginary axe to drop and chop off their new title as director.

D. Reck rarely made changes and was always happy when I got one of his features. Once he cut his teeth at Supreme and they began to dick him around and try to control him, he left with his newfound confidence. Once a new director realized that the killer in the horror movie that had been threatening them was really a Napoleonic troll under a sheet with two holes cut out, their confidence went up and they bolted out the front door. They could use the front door.

Next was Charlie M. His work was bright and exciting and he never truly looked over my shoulder. He trusted me. Yet he had that same 'looking over his shoulder' look they all did and he had been there for a couple of years. My desk was at the end of the room and he, and every other director, would lean on the wall and half face me but keep an eye on the door. Assuming they were waiting for the dictator and his mighty sword.

When there was an HIV scare in the industry, most high end companies went 'condom only' for their shooting sets. Also, the entire industry would halt production until the all-clear was called by the industry testing agency. This means that patient zero had been found and all parties contacted. Often, companies stayed 'condom only'. It made sense to me. Performers were the commodity here and they were the cash. They needed protection! Literally and… dickly. Supreme opted to be 'condom only' briefly but knew that shoots with condoms would simply not sell as well. Supply and demand, it seems, won out. Soon, they went 'condom optional'. Meaning, the actors could decide if they wanted to use them or not. This freaked Charlie out.

He came to my desk, leaned on the wall, and couldn't catch his breath. He looked pale and scared. For a man his size, over six feet tall with a large beer belly, it was really odd. He was clearly running from the killer in the horror film and thought he was the next victim.

"I don't want to lose this job but I can't be with a condom-optional company." He said, looking over his shoulder as he whispered to me. "I don't want to leave either but I think I have to." He was a 'condom only' advocate and all his shoots were condom only. He was truly distressed.

Or, that was how he presented himself to me. Let me pull back the curtain for you. Step right into Porn Hippocrasy.

Charlie's next shoot was with the 'condom optional' rule in place and was to be his last for Supreme. He had a man and woman having sex on the back of a car. Not in. On the closed trunk of a white sports car. It was a brightly lit scene with a white background and seemed to be going well. It was stylized and looked classy, for two naked people screeching like banshees on the Turtle Wax. The camera stopped and when it restarted I noticed something rather odd. In the close-ups of the action, there was no condom. There was only the ring of the condom on the guy's penis so it looked like he had on a condom in wide shots. I didn't use any close-ups for that scene. I didn't question Charlie. My suspicions were confirmed by someone who was at the shoot about the deception.

"Oh, yea. He does that all the time." The person said about Charlie and his shoots. All of his shoots.

Everyone has to make that money somehow, y'all.

After several years at Supreme, I began to get restless. I was editing features in record time for SJ because I knew how he shot. It got to the point that when I handed him a DVD screener, he would take the disc, physically look at it then hand it back.

"Looks great." He would say with a smile, not play the disc, and move on.

I would get handed a feature on Monday and then, as a joke, the post supervisor – still Roberto - would walk by my desk on Wednesday and ask if I was done.

"You got that new SJ thing done yet?" He would smirk like a frat boy about to make a dirty joke. Complete with looking over his shoulder at his pals for confirmation that he was cool.

"Yes, about to finish the cable version today." I would say flatly. His smile would fade.

"Nu uh. Show me!" He pouted and pushed me out of the way to look at the timeline on the computer. "Oh. Okay." He said as he left, defeated.

Obviously, I was getting bored. About this time, I decided I didn't want to be locked in an edit bay for the rest of my life. I went to the annual Vegas convention (on my own dime. Please, we couldn't have coffee and this place was going to give me tickets or a hotel room to a convention?) Not to mention the look of utter 'What the hell are you doing here?' I got when I went to the Supreme booth. I would find a nice seat and settle in to relax between laps of the convention floor and it was like a homeless person had come into their midst. As much as I would be tolerated at the office, here I was simply ignored. Only by staff, the female performers loved me, and one year, I spotted a non-sex actor I truly admired. SJ had done a version of Don Juan where Don Juan was an actor and this guy played Don Juan's agent in the feature. It was an updated version of the story, of course. His acting was so good. Once I saw him in action, I began to look for him in other features. He was wonderful in every role. Non-sex only. He would play the lawyer, the father, or the doctor. All without ever having sex on camera.

When I saw Frank Bukkqwyd at a booth at the convention, I walked right up to him.

"I am your biggest fan!" I said and handed him one of my business cards and told him who I was. He was flattered and shocked. "I am starting a fan club for you, you are awesome!"

We have been friends ever since.

Quick side note: I had asked Supreme for my own business cards and they flatly refused. I printed my own the next day with my own company name on them for what would be my freelance work. My 'company' was MasterWorx. I was the only employee.

Since the convention was only once a year, I knew I had to get out more. Supreme was having a release party at the Roxy in Hollywood for larger movie. I honestly don't remember which one but I am sure I edited it. Frank said he was going and would I like to join him. I jumped at the chance! I showed up in a dress that was so short, my ass stuck to the pleather booth when I sat. I saw many people from the Supreme offices and greeted them warmly. I always made sure to make friends in other parts of the company. Especially any females as I was the only one in editing.

I joined Frank in a half-circle booth and he introduced me to Tod Hunter, a writer for AVN. I shook his hand and my life changed.

Tod was a long-time AVN writer and went to every event in town to cover it for the magazine. This was the time when industry parties happened up to three times a week. Older and distinguished, we would spend hours babbling about a certain popular theme park, the one with ears, game shows, and old movies. He used to work in mainstream on a major quiz show. It will be the third thing he will tell you about himself behind the fact that he writes for AVN. The second thing? He will tell you I am THE editor in the industry. He was my cheering squad. He was tall and handsome, with a warm smile and soft voice. Everyone was always happy to see him since he was respectful to the performers, executives, and directors alike. He wrote all his notes in a small red spiral notebook. It was his trademark and always at his side. Once I met him, I didn't let go. I made sure I was at every event as his plus one. At first, people thought I was his wife!

I introduced myself to absolutely anyone that would take my card. I tossed them around the industry like ninja stars hoping one would stick. Several did and some porn performers that were trying to make the move to directing would have me edit their work. With these features, they could shop themselves around for directing work. Once they got a deal with a company, they would drop me flat and use someone they were told to use if they wanted to work for that studio. But more about Moralle later.

After eight years at Supreme, I asked for a raise and was told not at this time. When I saw the owner start to drive a different Bentley every day (he wasn't sure what color he wanted) I got personally mad. This was my fault. What he does with his money is his deal but we were working on AVIDs that were close to ten years old yet told to up our game. They did get a new AVID... one. Yes, one. The rest of us got low-end iMacs with Final Cut Pro on them. One DV deck for tapes that we had to share. It was like a cage of rats being tossed bread crumbs. The cover broke on the DV deck on day two.

The edit bay reminded me of a version is Scrooge. We were the family that refused to go to the workhouses and huddled around a trash can fire fighting over a potato that fell off a truck.

"No, you have it." One would say. "You have to work with that new director."

"No, I insist." As I passed the potato to the next man who was also balancing a dozen compilation tapes. "You have 30 comps to do before 5pm. You'll never make it." I would say and lay a reassuring hand on his shoulder. We would all leave the small fire and watch the man carrying the tapes throw himself into it.

I was asked to edit personal videos of the owner and his family. This was after I didn't get the raise. Maybe he thought me getting a glimpse into his life was a reward?

"Oh look, he has the Versace sheets on his double King bed!" I would gasp. "Fancy!"

We needed animal safari footage for a feature. I suggested buying some stock footage I had found. I was told to use the footage the owner had shot on his safari with his baby mama. I got to see their tent as they were 'roughing it'. The 'tent' included indoor plumbing; toilet and shower with hot and cold running water and HBO. The baby mama used the hair dryer daily before they were taken on their tour. I also got to edit footage of the baby. The baby was learning French at 8 months old. Then I got to edit footage of the owner's cousin HAVING a baby! That was a true gem.

"Hey, don't push, I have to get the camera in place." I could hear the owner and swore I saw a lighting crew rush in as his cousin was spread eagle on the table and very very very dialited. Wasn't I lucky?

The room was also filled with other family members sipping champagne and having some sort of cocktail party. Everyone was asked to wave. The baby popped out while the woman screamed to high heaven. I heard golf clapping and glasses clinking. Maybe they'd get the baby a Bentley. I edited this before lunch. I ate light that day. And couldn't look the woman in the eye again. She worked in sales on the first floor.

I was pretty close to quitting when the remake of an iconic classic came across my desk. Okay I said: One more film. And, it was shot on film. The remake of The Devil In Miss Jones with Jenna Jameson and Savanna Samson.

This was to be my second award.

The director, SJ, used small amounts of film because he could get the ends on the cheap. This was the norm. Once shot, he would have the footage transferred to Beta tapes and I would digitize those into the AVID. Thankfully, they transferred every inch of that film. One trick I used to edit the movie was those ends. The last few frames would capture a quick gesture or a look then it would flash to some burnt orange or white color and then be gone like a magician's flash paper. People nowadays pay to buy these effects. I had them for free. I used them all and they added a wonderfully creepy element to the film.

Savanna, as Miss Jones, was blonde and beautiful and a wonderful actress. She was also thinking of leaving the business when this film came in and she had to do it. She was also cultured and intelligent. The press went out about the movie as I was cutting and she went on a popular radio show to promote it.

"So, did ya do a snake?" the interviewer asked her point blank. Savanna stammered a little and said no, she hadn't.

In the original movie from the '70's, the actress has sex, somewhat, with a small snake. I have never seen the entire scene but I have seen enough.

A shoot was hastily arranged the minute she returned. I remember going through the raw footage.

They had Savanna on a bare mattress in an empty loft space. Light sliced through the slats of the abandoned area from the top and underneath making it nightmare-like. The mattress was lumpy and looked old with faded blue and white stripes. The scene was supposed to be a bad dream. She was naked on the mattress and the snake wrangler started to put dozens of different snakes on the mattress and on her. They ranged from small to size of a Buick. Now, her major phobia? Snakes.

She was told to writhe around and sort of make out with the snakes like it's the best sex she's ever had. These things were massive. One was as long as she was tall and it slithered up her entire body. She lifted one or two and attempted to kiss them. She recently told me that some of them relieved themselves on her. She wriggled and moaned between bouts of shivering and looks of total terror and revulsion. The snakes began to get away. They started to head for the slats in the floor. The PA kept grabbing them and physically throwing them back on top of her, often from several feet away so they landed on her body hard. Her body bounced on the mattress as the larger ones landed.

At one point, the largest cobra was over it. Once he was tossed back on Savanna, he raised up between her legs, flushed his head and hissed. Savanna let out a scream that I can still hear to this day.

Production was halted instantly and the snakes were put away quickly. Savanna went to her knees and hugged herself. The camera that had been shooting was set down hastily, still running, and I had a perfect view of her. In the background, you can hear people high fiving and asking 'did we get it?' and saying 'that's going to look great!'. Savanna was alone on the mattress, shaking. Her long blonde hair was damp with sweat as she hung her head, chin to her chest, covered in snake urine.

Five full minutes later: "Oh, someone should check on her." A distracted voice said.

A female PA came into the frame and covered her shoulders with a blanket and she collapsed onto the mattress. The camera finally cut but not before I watched her entire body shiver and heard her sob softly.

A month later, Savanna came into Supreme specifically to see me. She pulled up a chair, her eyes wide.

"Show me the scene?" She asked.

"Oh, you don't have to see that, hon," I said.

"I have to. Please?" She asked breathless and shivering as she set down her purse. Her eyes were wide and a little scared as he scooted close to me to see the monitor.

I put up the scene and she held my hand. The scene had been edited already and I added extra hissing but no music yet. That would be done by another department. I used a few angles and some slow zoom ins and several close ups of her face in ecstasy then close ups of the snakes. By the end of it, I had my arm around her and she was shivering harder.

"It's really good." She said with a nod and wiped her eyes. "Thank you." She said as she hugged me. I told her about her scream and how it had upset me to hear it. She assured me she was okay. Then I told her I had used that scream. She wanted to see it.

At the very end of the movie, her character is in hell and her hell is never having an orgasm again. She is locked in a room with a man that won't touch her after she has spent the whole movie becoming sexually awakened. She is begging the man to touch her but he won't. The picture fades as her pleading goes on. Over the black frame, before the director's credit, I put in the scream. The one from when she was scared of the snake. Savanna started to cry again and so did I. I am right now as I write this.

"That is perfect." She whispered.

At the awards that year, it won everything: Best Art Direction, Best Cinematography, Best Editing, Best Screenplay, Best Director, Best Actress, Best Film, Best Supporting Actress and Best All-Girl Sex Scene.

When the dvd commentary was being recorded, we were given a real treat. I was sitting at my desk and I heard the flutter of excited voices come off the elevator. I looked over the partition to see an older woman, smiling brightly in a pale pink track suit complete with beret-like hat. Her husband, an elderly man using a cane, was in the same style suit, dark blue. It took me a minute to realize they were headed my way with SJ at their side.

"Sonny, I'd like you to meet Georgina Spelvin. The original Miss Jones." SJ said proudly and the older woman held out her thin hand and shook mine firmly.

"I've seen the trailer and the latest cut of the movie, oh, you are wonderful. I love that a woman is editing this!" she gushed smiling at me, then hugged me.

I gave her the story about the snake scene and she gasped.

"That poor girl, but the scene was perfect," She said. Then she glanced at my non-linear editing system, fascinated and smiled "You know I started out doing this." She twirled her hand as if turning a crank, I realized she was mimicking tuning a film reel on an old edit station.

At the award show that year, I was on the outs with management. Mostly because I was still being judgemental about the owner and the way he treated us and I wanted that raise and wasn't playing ball about it. I was told that the owner keeps all the awards for his showcase because it is considered a company award.

The year before I had been welcomed at the company table and did get to physically keep my award. This year, I sat near the door and put on my running shoes.

When I did win, my friend Walter - tall, black, male friend - grabbed my hand and dragged me to the back of the room.

"Get your award, girl!" He said. I glanced and saw a Supreme sales person making a beeline for the award table. I got there first and physically clung to hard earned hunk of lucite. My heart was pounding out of sheer panic. Would I have to wrestle it out of someone else's hand? Why wasn't I allowed to have this one? Oh right. I was judging the owner. I saw the Emperor without his clothes. I was obviously in the wrong and had to be punished. No coffee for me!

"The owner wants that." The salesperson said.

"He didn't do the editing," I said to the salesman. "I did. I'm sorry." And I walked out shaking like a leaf. Everyone who saw me holding the award bought me drinks. All night. I slept with it.

I woke up in the morning and the award was on the opposite pillow in my hotel bed. I reached over to gently stroke the engraving that spelled out my name.

"How do you like your eggs?" I whispered and lit a cigarette. We've never been apart since that night.

After that, SJ started to push the boundaries with his filming. Stepmothers and step-siblings etc. are all the rage now but no one realizes that SJ did it first! I was editing a movie with two female actresses' and one male. One female was supposed to be the stepmother of the younger girl. Younger? They were pretty much the same age. Even during the filming, the older actress looked directly at the camera every time she said the words 'stepmother' to reinforce the ridiculous relationship.

It was hysterical!

According to management, I had to cut it all out and it ruined the film. I was one more foot out the door.

The corners they were cutting were indeed making me mad so I took on some freelance work. I wanted to! I wanted to be famous and I wasn't going to do it in the edit bay. Besides, editors are not famous. I was going to change that. Once Supreme found out I was doing freelance, they asked me to stop. Now, I was punching out at 5pm with the new thumbprint clock so when I was off the clock, this was my time. So, I tried to compromise. It was like playing Family Feud.

"We surveyed the two people that sign your paycheck. The answers are on the board." The game show host puts his arm around my shoulders and I stare up at the huge electronic board. I take a deep breath.

"Okay, then. How about a raise?" I ask, hopeful.

Survey says: Big red X. I try again, determined.

"How about you put me on a contract? Then I won't be an hourly employee, I will be exclusively yours." I cross my fingers and glance at the host's moustache.

Survey says: Big red X. I forge on!

"How about I get a promotion to post supervisor?" I close my eyes tight.

The survey says: Big red X. That was three strikes!

"Oh so sorry." The host says as he turns me back to the audience of two. "None of those answers are right. Have a good night folks and, Sonny, don't do freelance."

After that, I had my freelance clients deliver any footage to me at the front office. Even though I had to collect any tapes or hard drives through the side door.

After a year of that, the surveillance cameras came into the offices. There was one directly over my head at my desk. I wore a lot of hats, physically. Big picture garden hats like Lydia in Beetlejuice. Seems the owner watched the video feeds from his home before he came in the morning. He checked on all of them and if he saw something he didn't like, he would call his secretary and ask what was going on.

People were sleeping when they were supposed to be doing QC? Nothing.

People having one too many smoke breaks? Nothing.

But me? I had a flip phone and I would play endless games of Jewel Match while hour-long tapes digitized. We had no assistant editors. I knew they were watching me when I heard the owner asking 'who is she texting all day?' I was the reason the cameras had gone up. I should have practiced my stand up! Maybe done some card tricks for him! Tap dance!

I voiced my frustrations in my personal online blog. I never once mentioned the company. Still, Roberto found it and brought it to their attention. Since I never mentioned the company name, the admitted they had no leg to stand on but please don't do it, don't express your opinion. Oh, and don't do freelance. For his loyal service of ratting me out, they fired Roberto a year later after I left. He was so painfully loyal he never saw the boot coming to his head courtesy of the audio guy. Roberto had taught the audio guy how to worm his way into the owner's heart and he did it well. The owner liked sparkly new technology that would make the company look good as long as we used the lowest, cheapest, form of it. The audio guy also made sure the owner got rid of anyone the audio guy didn't like.

For the record, the audio guy was so cruel to me, that I won't even give him a fake name here.

When I gave my two-week's notice, the audio guy called me names for three days. SJ even called me names for three days because he felt I had bit the hand that fed me. I tried to talk to him a few times but he only ever resorted to calling me the 'C' word repeatedly. Then he would call my phone. It would start with an apology then the name-calling would happen. It crushed me to no end. I have no jokes or funny quips to add here. It just plain hurt. They were allowed their opinions but I was not allowed mine. My opinion got me kicked in the head, repeatedly. When I wasn't respected, I was just supposed to take it. They were right and I was wrong and that was that. They are all men, I might add.

As I was editing my final SJ film in those last weeks, SJ had another outside editor sit with me in case I sabotaged his feature. I have no idea how he thought I would do that. I had never done such a thing in my entire career nor would I ever no matter how much I might dislike the company I work for. The guy was very nice but confused as hell and liked my work. He made no suggestions to change any edits. I was being bullied for daring to have an unpopular opinion about the great and powerful Oz. Even a former Supreme Babe who I thought liked me, I found out recently she didn't because I had said bad things about the owner. She had played ball but had still been let go, she had dared to get older and he stopped hiring her but she still kissed his ass as other stars past their prime got directing deals. She was shown the door. But I was in the wrong. Right or wrong, I was allowed to have my opinion just like anyone else I simply wasn't supossed to say anything out loud. But being called a bitch and cunt by directors and coworkers, with no recourse just wasn't right.

I brought the name-calling by SJ and the audio guy to the owner and his secretary. I was given a very nice severance and I left a week early.

I was in the owner's very fancy office, noting the Keurig coffee maker he had set up near his desk. As he sipped his mochaccino, I stood and shook his hand, and thanked him.

"Oh and by the way I am walking out the front door." I smiled, and I did.

Years later when I was inducted into the AVN Hall of Fame, AVN gave me seats a few rows from the stage. I sat with Tod Hunter who had put my name in for consideration and looked around at the other inductees. Most were performers and directors I knew or had worked with. I was the first editor to ever be put into the Hall of Fame. Also, the first woman editor.

As I sat and settled in, I realized SJ was right behind me. Last time I heard his voice, he had been calling me the 'C' word into my voice mail. Time had passed. I felt a gentle hand on my shoulder and I turned to look into his eyes.

"Hey, congratulations. You deserve this and you've earned it. And, I'm sorry." He patted my shoulder and sat back, smiling at me sadly.

I nodded my thanks and smiled. I had finally earned what I really wanted, his respect.

CHAPTER SEVEN

I made a massive effort to meet anyone and everyone I could as often as I could. When I knew someone important was coming into the office, any office, I would just happen to be in the kitchen or near that front door. I would just happen to be the person to find the owner for them. Wasn't it lucky I was there? Oh, by the way, I'm Sonny. Nice to meet you! See you soon! Here is my card.

The cool thing about trade shows for me was that I never had to stand in line. I would always just cut to the front, hug the girl I wanted to see, then usually plop my butt in their booth and relax until I got my energy back.

I started going to trade shows and award shows as soon as I could. I never had to pay, which was nice. One year I was even on a panel at AVN. It was a panel about how production in porn works.

I was on the stage with three other people, men. One was an up-and-coming soon-to-be famous director. He was next to me. He smelled nice, I remember that. Like he found a men's magazine before he came in and opened a cologne ad to rub over his chest.

Most of the questions kept coming to me since I was post. How much footage am I usually handed? Is the director with me when I work? How much time do I spend editing? Actual real questions. I am sure it also helped that I was a rare approachable female in this sausage fest. The director on the panel kept shifting in his seat. By the end of the panel, he sort of looked at me like I had crashed the event.

"Hi," I said and handed over my card. "Big fan. Nice to meet you. Call me if you need me." I said, smiling.

He shook my hand and turned back to the other guys like I wasn't there. When I left the stage, the other three guys stayed behind and huddled to talk. About what, I don't know. I was shaking hands with the guys in the audience who had asked me the questions and they bought me a few drinks. They didn't hit on me, they wanted to know how it all worked.

And that director? Once he was famous, he picked out his new car from a line delivered to the front of his house. Posted the whole thing on social media. Total class.

At another AVN trade show, one of the AVN staff came to my rescue in a way I will never forget.

I was at the award show and had met some civilians that bought a VIP room on the second floor of the venue. That's what we call people who are not in the adult industry but who attend the events; civilians. I was bouncing all around but for the show, I went up there. See, at the Hard Rock, the free seat I got was way in the rafters (which I understood and was grateful for the ticket!) but I only ever sat there once during any show and that was for ten minutes. I had friends that would bring me to the first few rows or we copped a seat at tables in the back that rich people bought and paid for and never showed up.

In the VIP room I met a nice couple and we talked for the night. The wife got very very drunk and I helped her to the bathroom to throw up. Yeah, fun right? When I went back to the VIP room, my purse was gone. Gone. It had my car keys, wallet, phone. I freaked out.

Hard Rock security couldn't find it and I spent the rest of the night being a blubbering mess. I managed to get to my hotel by the grace of an amazing sympathetic cab driver and ten bucks from a friend. I got into my room because I had left my marijuana ID card on the bed. It had my picture on it.

I called my partner and I was reminded to cancel my debit card. I tried to calm down but I was inconsolable. I was in shock and barely slept. I would fall asleep for seconds then wake up with visions of my car being gone from the parking garage and I would be stranded totally. The next day I went to the parking garage at the Hard Rock and when I saw my car was still there, I cried and hugged the bumper. Not kidding. I still have that car and I worship her daily.

The next day I spent two hours on the phone trying to find a locksmith to get me into my car and make me a new key. I had to at least get home. I know it was Sunday but this was Vegas. A twenty four seven kind of town, right? It still took a miracle to find someone and without any help from AAA. It would cost me $400. My partner had a spare key at home and could FedEx it overnight. I was too freaked and just wanted to get home. But, neither of us had $400 on hand. Cash. I had my checkbook but this guy said cash only.

I tore through the Hard Rock finding anyone I could to see if I could borrow the cash and write them a check. I probably looked like one of those people with wild hair wearing a sandwich board that read 'the end is nigh' as the crowd parted when I came through the casino. Word spread and I found a girl from AVN. She worked in their accounting department. She texted the troupes and within a few minutes she got a response.

"Sharan says to meet her at the ATM by Pink Taco." She said and popped her gum, unconcerned, staring at her phone and still texting.

"Really? Okay!" I said, bleary and shaking. I made my way to the ATM and there was Sharan. She was the editor in chief at AVN. She was a slight woman with dark hair and large glasses. Shorter than me and very sweet.

"You need help, yeah? How much?" She asked as she put her card in the machine.

"$400. I can write you a check." I said. I think I spoke, I may have screamed. I know I was crying.

"No no, pay it back when we get home. Back to LA." She said and punched in the numbers. "Hmm, I think $100 for me too. Just to gamble." She giggled and pulled out $500, handing me $400.

"I can't thank you enough." I cried and crushed her to me.

"Oh please, it's an honor to help Sonny Malone." She said and she meant it.

"You're serious?" I asked, wiping away tears.

"Yes, of course. I was told it was you and I jumped at the chance to help." She said, smiling. "Now, drive home safe." She said and hugged me again. Then her husband arrived and they went off to the casino floor. I stared after them as I had a death grip on the money in my sweating palm.

I paid for the key. The locksmith was lovely. I got behind the wheel, hugged it, and cried for another ten minutes.

Then I drove to Cynthia Divine's brunch on the other side of town. Cheer Squad was my current freelance client and every year, morning after the award show, she hosted a brunch at a place on the other side of town. More… much more about her later.

Once I got there, I was plied with tequila shots and heavy breakfast food. I was still shaking.

"It's okay now. Told you not to worry." Cynthia said, all but brushing my worry aside the same way she had the night before. She didn't want her brunch upset with drama unless it was hers.

I had found her and Moses, her boyfriend, at a cafe at the casino the night before and asked for her help.

"You're drunk, it will be okay. Go get some sleep." And she went back to her food, assuming I had simply misplaced my car.

"No, I'm freaked out. My purse is gone." I said, shaking. "My car could be gone I have no idea-"

"Oh yeah, drunk." She cut me off and laughed. I died inside as I was then promptly ignored.

She acted the same way at her brunch. Next to me was Jerri, one of her girls.

"Can you give Jerri a lift back into town, now that you have your key?" Cynthia said. I looked at Jerri who looked just as happy as I was to be there. We were both chewing the tines on our forks down to nubs. Seems her weekend had been just as eventful.

"If it's okay. I'll pay for gas." She offered, shyly. I said, of course. I liked the girl a lot. She was sweet and always talked to me. Of course, after our bonding sister's four-hour drive and talking all the way home trip, she rarely spoke to me again. It was weird. We stopped and filled the tank, then got some donuts and sped back to Los Angeles.

Took me months to pay back Sharan but she didn't care. It gave me an excuse to visit the AVN offices and see my friends there. My best friend there was Sherri.

Sherri was the sex toy reviewer. She was also another big girl, like me. We would talk for way too long about everything but the business. We became confidantes and it was really lovely to just see her! Sadly, with our schedules, we rarely saw each other outside of her office.

The fun part, of course, was the 'closet'.

"You need things." She would say and grab a large empty box and throw open two large metal cabinet doors. She would look things over then nod as the doors rattled from being whipped open so fast. It was filled with things she had to review or already had been reviewed.

"Lube, some handcuffs, this device is USB operated now. Ah, got some good books here." She would rattle off the goodies as the box got heavier and heavier. "Here's a pocket one! Nice and powerful! And a pretty pink color!" She would say gleefully as the pink rocket rattled around in the box, and the box would be full. Like, super full. She was Mrs. Claus and she was stuffing my stocking. "Here are some stockings!" Into the box they went.

"You sure this is okay?" I would ask as I strained to lift the box.

"Of course!' She would smile. I would often give most things to directors I was working with for their shoots. Not all of it, come on now. Some were Christmas presents for my friends! USB powered even! I kept the books.

Needless to say, I've seen a lot of porn. Too many naked bodies slamming together surrounded by some of the worst acting you have ever seen. But nothing will ever compare to seeing a hard core porn film on the big screen.

The company was The Sandbox and they had grabbed J Bone once he left Supreme. He was a good fit there. The company truly was doing big things and changing the fabric of the industry and J Bone was ripe for that.

Pirates of the Caribbean had been a monster blockbuster in Hollywood so of course the porn parody followed. I went to the premiere at the Egyptian in Hollywood. Red carpet, fire eaters and all.

The star of the movie had long blond hair and decent body so he was the 'rock star' of porn. He was also a super nice guy that made sure to say hi to me whenever he saw me across a crowded room. The year I was inducted into the AVN Hall of Fame, he was too.

I was on the convention floor saying hi to other folks when he plowed through the crowd to get to me. He gave me a big bear hug and we congratulated each other on our awards.

"Yep, there goes the end of our careers!" He joked. I playfully slapped his arm. I knew he was joking. He always joked.

I went to the premier with Frank Bukkwyd. We got our popcorn and settled into our seats. I am not sure what I expected. Maybe a trimmed down version? The movie started. There was the long-haired rocker dude being very much a pirate in his flowing shirt with his flowing long hair, and chest puffed out. His voice was deep and commanding over his crew on the deck of the pirate ship. His overacting was perfect.

My friend Frank stepped into frame, said his lines as the first mate. Costume was right and lines delivered to perfection.

Then, the blonde starlet of the month showed up. Well, her boobs showed up first then she followed. Her boobs took up half the screen and her voice was a shrill as Minnie Mouse on helium.

The audience could not stop itself from laughing even when they were not supposed to. I am sure it hurt her feelings.

Later on, more cardboard acting followed by genitals. Even the actress I used to edit with the intake of breath and the 'yeah, well' was in the movie and the editor was lazy and did not do her any justice. He left in all her mistakes in an unforgiving two shot of her and the girl she was going to have sex with. I knew I could have made her look stellar.

Did I mention this was a huge movie screen? Not to mention a classic movie theater. It had been built in 1922 and was where Hollywood's first movie premiere happened! I know porn used to be only on a big screen but this was insane. And very close up. I know guys have a thing about their size but when it fills the screen and has a red painted lipped female drooling on it, I got nauseous. Not to mention the girl/girl scenes. I razor bumps the size of basketballs. I lasted about 15 minutes before I left to find a drink. A big one. Basketball size.

We went to the after-party while everyone patted each other on the back and I drank to forget what I had just seen. I never went to another big screen premiere again.

I lectured twice at UC Santa Barbara. Yes, I really did. It was a Porn 101 class taught by a woman who ran film studies. The class had a different fancy name but everyone called it Porn 101. It was an easy lecture class for students, I suppose. She had every porn company owner and porn director up there to speak. I think it gave us all some level of being legitimate. I love the look people give me when I said I spoke there. Porn folks would look at me like 'Ooh, you so fancy. Isn't that just for producers?'

My lecture was more about editing rather than just porn editing. I had my clips from my favorite mainstream movies cued up as I compared them like I knew what I was talking about. But, I actually did know what I was talking about.

The questions from the students were intelligent and interesting. They had the standard ones about 'what do you cut from a porn film' to 'do you know Ron Jeremy'. But for most of, if not all, the kids this was an easy A. A gut class. Something they had to take to get that final credit on their roster. It was nice to be included with all the high mucky muck owners and famous porn people.

Okay, truth time. I didn't belong but in a good way. The rest of the guests that spoke were just rich people and 'here is how I made my money from fuck films while I pretend to myself I'm making high art'. I was an actual working post production person. She never had any other editors speak. Not camera people, music people, lighting. None of that. Just me.

CHAPTER EIGHT

Before I left Supreme, I had lined up another job as a Post Supervisor at Sweeties Productions.

It was a small company down near the airport with a long reputation. It was an adult website founded by Sweetie; now a porn star past her prime but pretending to be in her 20's. The place was small but I liked the vibe. Younger people worked there including a girl named Rainbow who was obsessed with color correction. I see the joke there but it's the truth.

Once I arrived and settled in, within a month, they hired another post person from mainstream who was going to 'change porn'. If I had a nickel for every time I heard that one! She started with decorating her office, for a solid month, from her Pintrest board and billed it to the company. Then she got to the rest of the offices. I am not kidding. Her office came first. I wasn't going to be post super after all. I was lied to from the get-go. Meanwhile the words 'Eat, Pray, Love' were plastered over her eggshell walls with copper-colored pillows on her beige loveseat.

Then she decided to see about this porn thing and how all this worked. I was shoved to the back seat instantly. I had more years in porn than the whole place combined but that didn't hold up. We did weekly online sex shows and when the girls came in to shoot, they were happy to see me. They knew me because I had taken the time to see them at shows and conventions and say hi whenever they came in to the Supreme offices. Something else the owner at Supreme didn't like. Here, they loved it. I was still shoved in front of a computer rather than be in the position I was hired for.

I tried to stand up for myself but it just didn't work. I even tried to angle to direct the live web shows but the new person did that, badly. This new person, by the way, sort of reminded me of a rabid soccer mom. She was all hype and energy but really had no idea what she was doing but always had a clipboard and a huge bottle of water with the word 'hydrate' in scrollwork on it. It was beige.

The new person they brought in thought this was some sort of a playground. I don't even know what she did before they hired her. But, I was also not allowed to ask or to question her ideas. Just jump up and down and clap and be supportive. She ran all over the place looking as busy as possible while I cleaned up after her to make sure things ran smoothly. It still took them over 12 hours to burn one DVD.

I lasted exactly four months. She lasted one month after I left. This place needed a revolving door.

I was called into a meeting that I thought was to learn new procedures and to be part of the team. The meeting was 'stop being mean to the supervisor'. Seems she saw my cleaning up after her as a threat. I tried to explain myself and what I was doing but was shut down mid sentence. And told to drink more water.

I walked out. Did I mention I walked out on my birthday? I got handed a card they all signed and a cake. I took the cake and left the card.

Then it was on to Fly By Night Productions. I think I found the ad on Craigslist. I am only mentioning them here because they were their name; fly by night. They really showed the true nature of the industry. They swooped into the Valley with money to burn, lit the bonfire, and when it was out they left. The had a massive booth at the trade show that year, had lavish parties and did one major film that swept the awards. Then, poof..

I worked on their swing shift on compilations of old scenes they had shot or purchased. It was truly a chop shop. Their offices were nestled in the crappiest part of the Valley between two auto body shops. They had all the proper set ups for a porn company: high-end-looking conference room with dim lighting and brass and glass tables and chairs, (that employees were not allowed to sit in), a

backroom warehouse for distribution, and older-than-dirt computers we had to use to make magic. Seems the place didn't know I was
working there so that was helpful. When they did, the head of post
said 'We've got Sonny Malone here! She needs to edit our features!'
I remember seeing the conversation through the bosses' window
from the editing room, rows of computers, and all of us pretty much
dead in the eyes. But this was a ray of hope, other editors knew I
would ask for an assistant and they all looked at me expectantly as
the conversation in the office got louder, punctuated by the post
super blatantly pointing at me.

I worked on one feature there but it was a mess. It was some
director they had promised the world to and handed them duct
tape and an iPhone with a cracked screen. Go shoot magic. The guy
shot all long shots with no decent lighting anywhere. The movie
was supposed to start with a woman running on a track in a sta-
dium. So he picked the nosebleed seats to shoot from at dusk. Then
he zoomed in the jogging figure, the shot boucing and blurry. I
cut it out and was told I had to use it. Even though the next shot
was her coming into a living room with a towel around her neck,
clearly coming back from a run. But he insisted on the unusable
and useless establishing shot. Sound was on separate tapes and had
to be synced up but the audio and video were different frame rates
therefore completely impossible to match up. They never gave me
another film. The director turned out to be the owner's brother so
anything wrong was, of course, my fault.

It was a true nightmare. I did go to their premiere party for their
one feature. Tod and I made our way high in the hills to some lavish
home, he was covering the event for AVN. Our car was taken by
a valet. I wore new shoes and another short dress (two mistakes I
have never made again) and we made our way through the party.
On a big screen TV, the owner, who looked like a squashed Mr.
Bean, and the other execs screened the trailer on a loop. I was having flashbacks to that first year with the execs watching my trailer

before firing me. The trailer was all flash and filled with actors no one knew. They were just 'new money.' A lap through the house showed us that no one lived there, they rented it only for the party.

They swept the awards and two weeks later, we were all fired. The circus tent rolled up and tumble weeds blew across the abandoned parking lot. Gone in a puff of smoke and an echoing laugh. The entire industry saw the money and pounded on their door. We had all been duped. The owner took the money he won from the gamble and left the table.

CHAPTER NINE

The guy who hired me at Old Guard (with rabbit ears) Porn was Kip. He had worked in the offices at Supreme before so when he saw my name come across his desk, he knew me and hired me. He was a too tall gay man and we clicked at Supreme right away. I arrived at Old Guard full of all the anger I had built up at Supreme and beyond. I had a short temper and took it out on people often, Karen style. I was called into Kip's office more than once about it and he was right. Not to mention, watching a family member fall ill at the same time didn't help my emotional state.

Old Guard was probably the easiest job I ever had. It started with me and one other editor and we only did cut-downs like I had done at WorkHorse only on a larger scale with nicer equipment. I strived to work on one of the many shows that appeared on the company's cable channel but it never happened. As more people were hired, I was promoted to post supervisor. Finally! And I was good at it!

My job consisted of getting to work around 5 pm since I was in charge of the swing shift. I would meet with the day shift and be handed a rolling cart with the tapes to be done that day. I would roll them to my desk, hand them out as the crew rolled in. Then sit. For 8 hours or more.

If there were any fires to be put out, I handled them. Anything technical or problems with tapes or getting into the tape room? I was there. I made a lot of money sitting on my ass. It was a blessing and a curse.

I like to think I was a good boss and those under me told me so. One kid had to share his car with his mom as hers had broken down. He asked if he could come in an hour later three days a week. Of course I said yes and he always got his work done. I never told anyone above me because this was my department and I know how management would have handled it. I took care of my team as often as I could. I had been them too often so I wanted to see them as people before I saw them as employees.

Since I didn't have much to do, I was outside smoking for an hour at a time. With this, I met the ladies of the Old Guard radio show. Ginger Lynn was a performer who had been huge in the 80's and I had met her at Supreme a few times. She often greeted me with open arms.

I met Nikki Hunter in the most interesting way. She was a bubbly redhead at the time. Large eyes and a big smile. I had on a slightly low cut top and was smoking outside.

"Hey girl!" Ginger said as she came out from the radio station door and I hugged her.

"Hey! How's the show going?" I asked and stood up.

"Great! This is- " She turned to introduce Nikki.

Before we could say anything, Nikki walked up to me, buried her face in my cleavage and proceeded to motorboat my boobs. She then lifted her head with a smile.

"Hi! I'm Nikki!" She said. "Pretty bra!" She noted and looked down my shirt.

From that day forward, if I knew I was going to see Nikki, I would wear a pretty bra. My partner often helped me pick it out.

When they had a guest cancel on the radio show, I would fill in. It only happened a couple of times but it was fun! Except, they expected me to actually masturbate on air. It was something they did themselves for their listeners. They asked if I would and both Ginger and Nikki eagerly looked around for a toy for me to use. Phallic rubbery things were shoved at me like a mother placating a crying baby. Here just take it! I thought they were kidding. They were not. I politely declined and watched them instead. Rather I checked my phone for twenty minutes. Could not get out of that room fast enough and they never asked me to masturbate again. Talk, yes.

You would think I might have gotten some social media following after being on the radio. I got one person. One. He follows me to this day. Love ya, Joey.

Since I was indeed in charge, I also had to fire someone. It was the one and only time I ever did it. Kip made me do it since I was the supervisor. Scary thing was, I had worked with this person at Supreme too.

I don't even remember his name I just remember Kip hiring him without asking me. I had a hand in the rest of the crew. When I saw who it was I made sure to be all smiles but I warned Kip behind closed doors.

"Um, you sure about this?" I asked Kip, sitting on the other side of his desk.

"Yeah, he came from Supreme too. He will be fine." Kip assured me while arranging papers and not looking at me.

"He was fired from Supreme." I said and Kip finally looked up.

The guy lasted three weeks. I watched him come in and do the same routine he did at Supreme. Read the paper. Have coffee. Do some work and make mistakes. Read another part of the paper. Make some more mistakes. Go home.

I sat him down to give him the news and he was cool as a cucumber. I was a mess.

"We have to let you go," I said as soon as I stopped shaking so much.

"Oh. Okay." He said. He got up, and folded his paper. Shook my hand after I gave him his final check and he left.

I was more freaked out about firing him than he was about being fired!

Since Old Guard was in a working mainstream studio, there was a soundstage. Just the one. VH1 used it for all the reunions of their reality dating shows. For me, as a fan, it was epic. I got to meet all the guys from I Love New York and several other shows. The best was Rock Of Love.

Since I had my Sunset Strip Tattoo connection, as I said, I knew all the 80's and 90's rockers. I was outside, having a cigarette as usual when a small cluster of clamoring people hustled by with Bret Michaels' in the middle. Poor guy was just trying to find a bathroom.

"Hey, Bret," I said from my bench outside the studio.

He turned and waved with a smile then stopped. He looked at me, pointed a finger, and blinked a few times.

"Sonny, right?" He said. We had met only a few times before. Couple of times at the tattoo shop then at a party for the Young Guns 2 premiere. "From Sunset. Your friend works there. How ya doing, girl?" He said. Then he detached himself from his crowd, came straight over and hugged me.

"Doing good. You?" I asked.

"Ah you know, doing the thing." He laughed. I pulled out my phone to take a pic.

"Gotta have proof I saw you." I laughed.

"Oh girl, we need one together." He handed my phone to one of his people and they framed it perfectly. We only chatted for another minute before he had to go. Bret was an angel.

Since the job was so deadly boring, I spent a lot of time talking to people in other departments. I asked if they needed an editor or was there anything I could do besides my current job. All was a big fat no. Speaking of fat, I gained more weight and smoked too much for three years.

I did spend a lot of time in the machine room with the operator there. His name was Ross and he was from Arizona. He was a big bear of a guy with a bright smile and a massive heart of gold. He had come to Los Angeles to be famous and we all know how that goes. Dreams are great but you can't pay the bills with them. He had a technical background so this was a logical step after a stint in radio elsewhere. He was also a background actor when I met him and we would talk about everything and nothing for hours. After I left, he made sure not to lose me and we are still friends. I had no idea how important he would be to my future.

I wasn't shocked when I got let go. The work was coming in less and less. They only kept two guys and I was being paid the most so it fit. I had freelance work, which I was doing at Old Guard (on my own laptop) while I was there. I knew money wouldn't be an issue but now, I was truly on my own.

CHAPTER TEN

Here is the reason I never got to direct. Several actually.

1 - I didn't inherit family money to start my own production company.
2 - I do not have a dick. I've checked.
3 - I am not on camera talent whose name would sell the feature.

Even though the camera guy really does the directing. In interviews, the starlet will bat her eyes and say something like: 'I've always wanted to direct'. Of course, her hands would be clasped in her lap so her boobs would be more prominent. "As a woman in this industry"…. Blah blah blah. I saw something recently about how porn has 'more female directors than Hollywood'. Bullshit. Straight up bullshit. It goes like this:

The female porn talent/director spends an hour in the chair getting her hair and make up done. She stays in her bright pink sweats with the word 'Juicy' across the ass and tip toes to the set even though she is in sneakers. She is used to hooker shoes.

"Okay guys, let's get started." She quips and bounces, script in hand as her pony tail swishes like a Barbie Doll.

The crew has been ready for two hours. Lights are in place and the set is ready.

"What's the first move, boss?" The direc… um.. camera man steps up and slips his hands into his pockets. The stills for the scene have been shot. Everything has already been plotted out and handled by the cameraman.

The blank stage has been dressed to look like a random bedroom. "Uuummm... Let's say they start here." She points to the pressboard Ikea dresser. "Ummm no... here." She points to the wobbly wicker chair next to the bed. She looks at the camera man and smiles brightly. "Okay?" She chirps. That was it. That was her directing.

"Sounds good." The cameraman says and does exactly what has been already planned. The cameraman tells the talent when to move, when to add more lights, tells the boom guy to stop scratching his ass and hold the mic still.

The female porn director spends the whole scene taking selfies and posting them '#directing'. The company puts her name and picture on the box as her 'directorial debut'! The cameraman pockets his fee and does 'camera work' for the rest of the girls in town.

Let me tell you about Porn Freelance rather than Real World Freelance. In porn, there are no contracts. There is no guarantee of money. There is only a handshake and verbal agreement.

It's like having a meeting with a pickpocket.

"Hey! How's it going?" As the director and freelancer are shaking hands, the freelancer's watch goes missing.

"Good, good, you?" Director hugs freelancer, pats them on the back, three buttons go missing from their shirt.

"Great. You want to edit that movie/shoot those stills/do that makeup for me?" Another smile from the director as the freelancer's wallet goes poof.

"Sure, meet my price?" Director sips his drink, freelancer's shoelace is gone and is wrapped around the glass.

"No, a little lower. C'mon this is me. Gimme the family price." Cheezy smile followed by more drinks, the freelancer's entire shirt is suddenly gone.

"For you? Anything." The freelancer agrees, smiles all around and the freelancer is naked. The director is wearing all your clothes as he slips through the party and you are doing the work for a third of the price and you won't get paid until a month after the project is complete.

Nine times out of ten, all is well. Because, if a director goes back on an agreement, word gets around lightening fast. I was often bullied by the directors I worked for and only really realized it writing this book. I would talk to other (male) editors and would hear how great so and so was and I would aspire and aim to work for these amazing directors. I would work with them and it would be a nightmare.

It was always interesting when a director/client came into my home then into my home office. It was like they did not blend with the vibe of the house. This was my home they were coming into. None of them fit. None of them looked comfortable and the atmosphere always crackled. They were Alice in Wonderland and their egos or personalities were too big to be contained in this small space.

Also, when I read a script, I can tell how the writer likes to have sex.

When the dialogue leading into the sex scene was complete, the actual sex to be shot was marked with the words 'commercial scene'. Now they are marked with 'B/G scene' (or whatever pairing it is; boy/girl, girl/girl, etc.) But when I see the script describe what needs to be done, such as 'she kisses his... or he touches her... ' then I know the writer wrote it because it is what they want to see. What they write is their kink. Ew.

It wasn't hard to find directors that wanted more control over their work so they would hire me. Problem was, I would make them look good, they would get a studio contract and have to use the studio's editor as part of their new contract. I can not tell you how many times I would hear 'you are my editor for life'. I was good for a half a dozen features or less. This is called Porn Loyalty.

My first freelance client was Richard de Monfort in 2004. I only did a movie or two for him but it gave me the freelance clout to gather more clients. He passed in 2009 and I was sad to hear it. I remember him in his trademark black outfit sitting in my studio apartment. He looked over my shoulder at my laptop screen as we worked. He paid on time. I liked him. His energy did fit my home.

My second client, the same year, was an established male porn star. He had long dark hair and movie star good looks. He was trying to break into directing like most performers do and he knew I was good and available. He was soft spoken even though he had a deep voice. He liked my work and I liked having him around. The year I knew him personally, he was clean and sober. I will explain this later. When I was close to finishing his second feature, he said he was going home for shoulder surgery. He had played sports professionally when he was younger and had some old injuries. His family was in Nashville and he was going to have the surgery and recoup there. He wasn't going to go until after the holidays and I asked him, earnestly, to spend the holidays with us. He politely declined but loved that I thought of him and had asked. The other joke we shared was when he cut his trademark long hair before the surgery. Honestly, it was hot. The short hair made him look younger! But when he cut it, he said he was worried how I would react to it. We met up at a party.

"Oh no! Don't turn around!" He said, behind me as I waited at the bar for a drink, his hands on my hips. Honestly, I leaned back into him a little and sort of stayed there for a second. Did I mention he was uber hot?

"It's okay. I won't freak out." I joked. I turned and smiled. "Oh wow! You look great!" He did. Having his hair short took years off of him.

We hung together a lot that night. He was talking about being nervous about the surgery but looking forward to seeing his family. He couldn't wait to get back to work when he returned.

They gave him pain pills after the surgery. He didn't direct another film. I didn't edit for him again.

Flash forward to a few years later and I saw him at a trade show. He had a tight smile glued to his face and his hair had grown back to his shoulders. When he used to greet me, it was with a genuine hug and warm welcome. This time, it took him a minute to focus.

"Hey there!" I smiled after I fought through the crowd to get to him.

He was… glazed…and looked at me for a long moment as I heard some gear turn in his head.

"Oh. Hey." Mechanical hug and stuck on smile. I don't bother to try to have a conversation.

Then there was Richard Shaw. He was a heavy set guy with a big smile and a huge heart. He was always happy even when things were bad. I edited a lot of things for him for The Old Guard before I worked there myself. What I didn't know was that his girlfriend was an executive at The Old Guard and made sure her boyfriend got monthly work. No matter if the work was good or bad or recycled. Seems it went on for years and I was just along for the ride. When The Old Guard figured it out, they fired her and they broke up. Sadly, Richard is no longer with us but he always made me smile. Also, I recently heard he used speed, complete hearsay of course. This is not totally uncommon in any industry but I am completely oblivious to it. Always have been. I can never tell if someone is fucked up or not or on what. I just don't have that filter. For the record, I still have the folders I made for the scripts of the movies I edited for him. He respected me and I will never get rid of those folders.

I got a call from a guy named Scott Slick in 2004. He worked with a female performer who had started her own company, like you do, and she needed an editor. He was the ultimate salesman and just a cool guy. He was shorter with dark hair and a wide smile. He was the kind of guy you could see in a loud plaid suit, chomping on a cigar, standing in a used car lot waving people in.

"Have you seen this? Ain't she a beauty?" He would exclaim and pat the bumper. The bumper would fall off and hit the ground. "Oh that? Don't worry about that, I got duct tape. Besides, it looks better this way! Lighter to drive around! How much to get you into this baby?"

The offices were former mainstream production offices that had a massive tree growing right in the middle of the lobby. I think I met the female performer/owner once. The editing was a breeze. It was nice to edit things with a female touch and I got paid well. Until she decided to go another direction. That means she got older, her movies were not selling, so she went back on camera as a MILF performer and shut down her production house to save money. Classic story.

Down the road, at one AVN show, Scotty was painfully hammered and hit on me so hard I almost fell over. Not even sure he was focusing on who he was trying to get to into bed. I just nodded a lot and gently pushed him towards his cluster of business buddies. He says he doesn't remember that night at all. We laugh about it now and he still calls me for odd freelance work now and then even though I never put out. That's the joke, people.

I went to every trade show, party and award show that would have me to network. Once I found Jay (of Jenna Jameson and Jay fame) and he smiled and hugged me. We met at Supreme several times.

"So, I have a question for you," I asked him as I palmed a business card of mine like a magician doing a trick.

"Yea?" He asked.

"Why don't I work for you?" I said and handed him my card. I almost used a top hat and pulled a bouquet of flowers from my bra.

He blinked a few times then smiled.

"I don't know. I guess now you do!" I edited for him and Jenna for a year.

I used the 'why don't I work for you' line a lot and often it worked! It was something I learned about sales from Scotty. Never ask a question you can say 'no' to, you always want a 'yes'.

You are in a shoe store picking up a pair of pumps and a salesman comes up.

Scenario one: 'can I help you with anything?' No.

Scenario two: 'isn't that a great color?' Yes.

"Do you need me to edit for you?" No.

"Why don't I work for you?" I don't know, why? And the conversation starts in the right direction. Even if the answer is ultimately no right now, down the road, I usually get a yes. That question laid important groundwork for my freelance career.

There was one male performer that needed DVDs burned. That was it. It was easy money and the guy was nice. He had an office in a run down industrial complex deep in the Valley. When you walked into the offices, the cloud of blue smoke was thick. Like walking in to an 80's music video. He had a woman doing his books that barely spoke English. When I asked for a check it was quite the ordeal and took longer than making the DVD. The place itself was dingy and the furniture was old. It crunched when you sat down.

The only reason I mention this guy is because when he moved out and moved on, a leasing company moved in. The leasing company we rented our house from! I had to look at the address twice when the leasing office gave me their new address. I walked in to pay the rent and the place had been totally redone! Hardwood floors and new bathrooms! It was spotless and extremely tasteful. I told them what had been there and they said they had to burn the furniture.

"Couldn't even donate it. They were living here!" One girl told me.

Another new director needed to get cash from his backer before the shoot and he wanted me to meet the guy. Having me was part of the package deal to fund the movie. I sincerely do not remember the director. We drove way up into the Hollywood Hills to a massive house overlooking the valley. Outside, it was modern and formidable. A concrete blockade that made you think of Russian spies in a James Bond movie. Inside, it was old and musty and looked like it hadn't been touched since 1973.

I met the backer. He was bald and older and smiled like a subway flasher when he saw I was a female.

"Could you look at some footage for me?" He asked seriously and led me to another room. His bedroom. I felt like the kid in Airplane talking to the pilot. He all but turned and said' 'you like movies about gladiators?'.

He flopped onto the bed, on his back, stretched out and grabbed a tv remote. Clicking it, a picture came onto the massive screen that took over most of the wall. It was a girl and two guys. It was Golden Showers video. I almost threw up.

He smiled at the screen and grabbed his dick through his pants.

"You like it? You can get into that right? You'd get off editing this." He asked, his voice low and gravely. I would rather have had the model of the airplane and a parachute.

I didn't say a word. I walked out, gave my director who brought me to this windowless hell a dirty look and waited in the car. I never worked for him again which is why I can't remember his name. I blocked it out. Things like that didn't happen often and I will bet it rarely happened to male editors. Just a hunch. Now take your seat, the captain has turned on the no harassment sign.

In 2007, I worked for Kimberly Cumbers. In my world, as I previously stated, we rarely sign contracts for money. It's a handshake. With her, I had to spell it all out. She often did the 'oh, I will get you a check next time' thing. She assumed we were pals and the weeks passed with no money as I worked. I stopped that pretty quick and she didn't like that I held her accountable. She was bankrolling all of this herself and I could respect that but I needed to get paid. I even got the press (Tod Hunter and others) to cover her shoots. One thing, she always hired a caterer for each movie set.

One shoot, my last for her, was running late. But, we were a team and we could get this done! I was there collecting footage as it was shot. The caterer put out fresh banana cheesecake to give everyone a sugar boost to get us to the finish line. I grabbed a plate with everyone else and dove in. It was freshly made and wonderful! Then, after two healthy bites, I started to feel strange. My head got dizzy and I was having trouble breathing. My friend Walter was there taking still photos (I had gotten him for Kimberly at a good price). He dropped his camera, grabbed a big bottle of water, and two Benadryl, and pulled me into an empty bedroom. The caterer was close by too. He did all he could do to help. Kimberly was… not around.

"Here, drink as much of this as you can and take these." He said, handing me the pills and water. I did as he asked and tried to take deep breath.

"Can't. Breathe." I stammered, getting scared as I grabbed at my throat.

"You're okay, it's just an allergic reaction. You're gonna be fine." Walter assured me in a soothing voice. He told me to drink the water and just lay down. He and the caterer kept checking on me while they shot the last scene.

I managed to drive home after the shoot but my muscles were seized up for two days. To this day, I can't eat bananas. I had no idea I was even allergic!

Go ahead and make the appropriate 'lesbian allergic to bananas' joke here.

Side story about the stills photographer: His name was Walter. He and I tried to start our own line of solo girl videos. It failed miserably but we had fun shooting! We shot at his house and got brand new girls for a good price. All solo stuff. We asked if we could add a shower or tub scene, paid of course, if they wanted. Some said yes, some said no. We always tried to be good to the girls. I was told over and over that solo doesn't sell. Yet, somehow, just about every company I talked to, pitching our video line, came out with their OWN solo line within the next year. I eventually sold the footage to a Canadian company for peanuts. Just like the rest of the industry.

However, that year, Walter and I attended AVN together to shop around the footage. No one was biting. It was my friend Nikki's birthday (Nikki Hunter of the 'motorboat' incident at The Old

Guard) and she invited us to her party at a high-end strip club. I had never been to a strip club and Walter frequented places like that often. So, we went.

We took a cab there and were ushered to the center of the large place under a round raised lucite stage. This was for Nikki's guests. The place was dark and the music was booming, shaking the walls. But, it was clean and looked okay. How would I know? I'd only seen strip clubs on tv and in Motley Crue music videos! We got to look up at the girls dancing. Nikki hugged me tight and made sure we had drinks. She had an unlimited tab for the night as she was the birthday girl and the star attraction. At one point, a sweet young girl with short blonde hair and wide blue eyes walked over to me and straddled my lap. She wearing basically dental floss and Life Savers as an outfit.

"Oh, no thank you hon. I don't want a dance." I said.

"Its okay, he paid for it." She smiled sweetly, nodding to Walter who was laughing and loving how uncomfortable I was.

"Oh.... okay..." I said and tried to relax.

"You can put your hands on me. Men can't, but you can. You're pretty." She said and pulled my hands to her tiny butt.

She looked 18 but was at least 21. She was adorable. The dance was short and sweet.

Half an hour later, a lovely black girl, with the same style of out-fit, and the same wide eyes, did the same.

"Walter says you need a dance." She said. "You can touch me if you want."

I wanted to strangle Walter.

But, what he did not count on was what happened next. The little blonde wandered back over and smiled.

"Hey, my feet are killing me. Can I sit in your lap? Its free. I just want a break." She said, biting her lip.

"Oh sure," I said and she sat. She refilled my drink and we talked about shoes and purses, my hand on her back to keep the men away while she rested. Also, this was while she was still on the floor so therefore her bosses approved. I glanced at Walter and his mouth sort of fell open. Then, the pretty black girl did the same thing. I wasn't without a pretty girl in my lap all night. Yes, Walter was jealous!

We decided to take the venue's limo to head back to the hotel. We were both pretty hammered, it was free, and I didn't want to join Nikki's 'after party' which I believe turned into a sex thing. Walter was married and I was with my partner so it wasn't our scene.

The limo pulled up after 45 minutes and a woman driver got out to open the door. She smiled. She was tall and beautiful with a chauffeur's hat and jacket wearing high heels. She looked like she walked straight out of an 80s music video with the hat set askew and black high-heeled pumps.

"Hey, saw you tonight. The girls loved you." She smiled as she helped me in.

"It was all his fault!" I giggled and fell into the back seat.

Walter and I babbled all the way back to the hotel and I thanked him for making my first time a strip club a memorable one. I didn't know it was going to be my only time at a strip club. I sipped the offered champagne and was ready to fall into bed.

When the limo arrived at my hotel, the driver turned to look at us.

"Stay there, you need the whole treatment." She smiled. My door was opened and she offered her perfectly manicured hand to help me out.

"Wonderful to see you again, Miss Malone. Hope to see you soon." She purred, smiling at me and Walter tipped her handsomely. I loved the looks of shock from the groups of bachelor parties as I got out of the strip club limo with style. Yes, I was someone.

I loved it when things like that happened. I wasn't a starlet or anything. I was a regular looking overweight female who happened to work in porn. It's something we as humans can not help. When you see a person, you judge right off. It's not personal, you can't help it. Its human. I know when people saw me their first thought was about my weight. It's what I had to touch on first when I did stand up. My coach made sure of it.

"It's the first thing they are going to see." He said. "It's not a bad judgment, but they will see the weight. Just as they would see your skin tone. Length of your hair, anything like that. So you have to address it."

My opening line was: 'So, I've decided to go back into porn." The crowd would always laugh because the idea of someone built like me being in adult films WAS the joke. I got it and I made the joke first.

When I would go to trade shows and see the long line of fans waiting to see the girls, I would walk past them to the front of the line. I would wave at the girl who would inevitably stop what they were doing and hug and talk to me. The looks on the guys faces was kind of priceless. Like, 'who is she?!'. Good for my ego, I think. I did it a lot.

I did edit a few features for a man I will call Big Time director. He was/is one of the biggest directors at Moralle and I was more than excited to be part of the team. It was the one company I fought the hardest to be a part of as it was still considered to be the most prestigious next to Supreme. Big Time Director was a short, stocky man with dyed black hair plugs and the slightest lisp. Oh yea, a true stud. I was doing compilations for him, nothing complicated. He seemed happy with my work and I liked working for him. He was a nice guy, briefly. They are all nice, briefly.

He handed me a movie that had a space-age theme because that's original, right? I did an edit with the music and handed it in. I liked it. It showed the girls as well as the set without being too gim-micky. The idea of these features is the girls and the sex. The rest is just window dressing. Then again, I think being at The Old Guard for three years maybe dulled my instincts.

He came to The Old Guard offices to pick up the screener then returned with my check and some notes.

"Its kind of dated. 80's style in the editing." He said, ruefully, and handed me a check instead of more work.

"Yeah but, you shot it 80's style," I said, half joking. Only half. It was girls in Spirit Halloween space slut costumes on a set made of sprayed silver cardboard with Christmas lights used on a console. But he expected Star Wars with boobs.

Often directors would not change how they shot but would insist the editors change everything about they way they edit. That's fair, right? New technology was on the rise and editors were coming in throwing every sparkly trick at the wall. Directors would grab the new shiny like a toddler, tire of it then grab the next shiny. It was the new way to do things. It would die out (and did) as all fads do, but for now it was the trendy thing. Moralle Studios liked being on trend.

Big Time nodded, got into his car, and left.

I never took it personally. Some directors and editors just don't mix. Although, we had been mixing just fine. It was odd. Pretty sure this is where my problems with Moralle started. I assume the big boss leaned on Big Time to somehow change how he did things as all of his movies were looking the same and he expected me to save his bacon. He shot it the same and I edited it as differently as the same footage would edit. Only so many ways to highlight a tacky looking 80's set with girls in tacky 80's style silver lemme space thongs.

Years later, I was at the AVN Convention wearing a shirt that said 'don't you know who I am?' (which, I really need a new one!). He said he liked it. I sent him one and said he could wear on shoot days. I have no idea if he ever did.

2010. Staying with Moralle, I started to work for Bryan Salte. He was a performer turning his hand to directing and he was the biggest Dude-Bro you will ever meet. Spiked thinning hair with frosted tips. Always wearing tank tops one size too small to show off his muscles, or rather lack thereof. Over suntanned. Wallet with chain attached to jeans. Started nearly every sentence with 'dude'.

'Talking Trash' was my favorite movie with Bryan. It was a subtle take off of an old Christian Slater movie. We just had fun with it! He loved the timing of my work and he said the sex editing was stellar. He seemed really happy at this point in our relationship. I did five features or more with Bryan.

After a couple more movies, he used this phrase a lot:

"I really fought to keep you on this one. You're my girl."

Now, at the start, I was touched. I was wrought with Daddy issues so having a male figure in authority talk to me like this, I would have given him a kidney. I didn't realize that was what he wanted. Undying and unwavering loyalty at a super low price. Figured out that was the real reason he kept me, and I stayed below his budget. Yes, I was good but as he got more money for each feature, I never saw it. Also, he needed a scapegoat. If something went wrong, he could look at management and say: "Yeah, you were right. I shouldn't have used her. But next time… "

I didn't find this out until later.

One movie Bryan shot was during the Mean Times at Moralle. What that means is that every single frame of every feature was scrutinized for any kind of logo or label infraction of any kind. It was yet another time we thought the government was going to find any reason to stop porn. They never did but these big companies ran scared every time. Happened like clockwork every ten years.

Everything starts with that blood draining phone call.

"Dude, we got a problem."

Next thing I know I am in Moralle's offices going over Bryan's new film with Bryan there. He shot a movie about working out at a gym and every single actor had a logo on their shoe or their underwear or their shirt. Every. Single. One.

I wasn't called out for missing it. Bryan was called out for film-ing it. I was taxed with fixing it, which I did. It was basically a 100% painstaking re-edit with making shots larger to cut out the logo, or just cutting the shot completely. Just flopping the picture to make the logo appear backward was no-go. No, I was not paid more by anyone. Bryan approved every edit and Moralle threw it back three times. I was getting bleary eyed. Eventually Bryan just threw me under the bus.

"I don't want have to watch these things, dude. Trusting you to take care of this stuff."

Basically:

"Dude, I fucked up. But you'll take the fall right? You're my girl, dude."

Directors don't watch their work. Ever. They collect the money and blindly shoot and just want it done to get to the next feature. A few do watch their work but the majority just want that dollar bill.

I was at the Moralle offices a lot for a while working with several directors. They had an in house editor as well. This place is another perfect example of 'playing at being a company'. Not legally. Legally, they had it all together just like the other big places. But this place looked like it sold auto parts, just like the rest. Junky 70's looking furniture in a tiny lobby with crappy carpet. The logo on the wall was bigger than the room. They had it made for AVN and their booth and rather than store it, they hung it up. When you went to the back offices, it looked like a fire sale at a 60's office building. Cheap desks and cheap IKEA chairs. The edit bay was laughable. It was tucked inside the back door in the space of a closet. Cheap indoor/outdoor grey carpet from the floor tacked on the wall to make it 'soundproof'. But like all these places, they have a HUGE conference room. All brass and glass and a wall crammed with awards illuminated with swanky lighting. The owner's desk, like all of them, was covered in random papers with more awards behind their heads. Family photos of their kids next to stacks of DVDS of

Babysitter and Step Mom movies. Seriously, walk into any Pep Boys and look at the boss's office. Identical. Maybe not the porn DVDs but you get my point.

This is where Bryan and I went south.

I was dealing with the death of a close family member but still had to keep a roof over our heads. Bryan had gotten me work with Lord Nique. I had always wanted to work with Nique and jumped at the chance. Then the job was presented to me as 'well, I can't pay much but later it's gonna be a butt load of money!' This is the free-lancer's code for 'RUN! Run NOW!' I took the job anyway but I was not in my right mind.

As I sat on a couch in a dingy studio, waiting for the files to transfer to a hard drive, I started to fall apart. If I sat still too long, my brain would start to run over time and my heart would break thinking of this lost family member. This room was just depressing and you know someone just had sex on the wobbly desk that Bryan was sitting at it with his laptop. My feet stuck to the carpet and I was getting ill from the yellow walls, yellow floor, yellow furniture combo. I was keeping it together as best I could as I was dealing with heavy grief. I was texting my partner and telling her I could not do this. She assured me I would be okay.

Bryan was at the desk when Nique came in. Came in and didn't even acknowledge I was in the room five feet away. I realized, Nique was a Dude-Bro too. They each actually SAID Dude-Bro to each other a few times while they spoke in extremely derogatory terms about the girl that had just left. She was a new performer and they were saying her breasts were too small and she was too scared. Then some more things about her vagina etc. all while playing with the large silver rings on their fingers and fussing with their wallet chains. Yes, Nique had the dude-bro spiky hair but it was dark and not high-lighted. I started to tune them out or I was going to start screaming.

Then Eric Masterson, a performer who was filming a scene later that day, came in and sat on the couch. I had known him for a long time, actually met him when I was at Porn Town years before and we were casual friends. Always hugs at parties and conventions. I was crying a little and just trying to get through. The Dude-Bros pretty much forgot I was there. Eric reached over and touched my arm gently.

"You okay, hon?" He asked. His eyes were honest and looked worried about me.

I nodded and then briefly told him my story. He knew the person in my life that had died.

"Stay right there." He whispered. He jumped up, got me a bottle of water and some tissues immediately. He sat back down, sitting closer, and rubbed my back gently. He stayed with me, talked to me, and made sure I was okay. The Dude-Bro conference was unfazed.

"I'm here if you need me." Eric said softly, reminding me that I had his number if I needed to talk. I adore him. He does not know how much that meant to me. I hope he reads this and finally knows he saved me that day.

I talked with Nique out by his car before I left. We talked about the project and I was getting his vibe on things. We seemed to click just fine. I had a deadline of February 1st.

I started editing. It was a simple two camera shoot and when I was done it was to go the special effects guy for finishing. Let me say again, I should not have taken on this project. I was being paid well below my rate but I wanted to work for Nique and I wasn't thinking straight. I was buried deep in grief over the death in the family that I am sure my work suffered.

Three days before the due date, Nique called me.

"WHERE'S THE EDIT?!" He screamed at me over the phone and I went ice cold. Yes, screamed.

"It's not due for three days." I stammered.

"I have to get it to my effects guy! Its due to the STUDIO on the first!" He yelled. I wasn't given that part of the information so this was my fault. "Besides, what you sent was totally unusable for our effects guy. Do you even know what you are doing?"

At this point, I just started to cry. I should have hung up and told him to go to hell. I ended up backing out of the project at his suggestion.

"Bryan and I can do this faster and better. We will just have to handle it." He said, mad as hell.

I agreed and hung up. I wrote it off and started to delete the files. I wasn't ready to go back to work anyway, I needed some real time to grieve.

The next day he called me back.

"What sort of editor are you? Have you zero integrity? Bryan vouched for you and this is what you do?" He yelled.

The tirade went on for ten minutes. I was shaking and close to throwing up. He bullied me into taking the job back. I was so confused I didn't know what to do.

The following day, he called again.

"Just leave it, we got it. I will pay you for your time. Send me an invoice." Click.

I got paid six months later. I avoided him at every trade show and party. I never heard from Bryan again.

Yet somehow, Bryan entered my world through Tessy Waters. She was a new starlet starting her own production company, as they all do. She had hired Bryan as cameraman (director, whether she knew it or not) and when she asked around about who to hire to edit, she was told my name over and over. That made me feel good. Especially after being verbally beaten up by Nique.

She was a sweet girl with good ideas and an apartment that looked like the Hello Kitty aisle at Toys R Us. All pink. Smelling like the bubble gum section of Yankee Candle. She was very nice and paid on time. I really have nothing bad to say about her. She was wonderful to work with! She just stopped making her own movies. She did insist I have DVD copies of all the movies I edited for her. She was shocked that no other client did that for me. I didn't have the heart to tell her the DVDs were just barter fodder for brake jobs.

Often female performers would want scenes edited for their own website. Many were tired of waiting to be hired and started to strike out on their own. Once being a Cam Girl went big, no one needed editing at all anymore. Cam Girl meaning you work from the safety of your home on a webcam. Safe, secure and you make your own hours.

But before then, I would hit the trade shows and talk to the girls as much as the directors. One girl was Little Sally.

I met her at a convention in Los Angeles. The guy that ran the trade show was/is a total douche. He didn't want people to network inside the show so he never gave out free passes. Also, when I was searched before I walked in, my stack of business cards were confiscated and set to one side. I was sort of shocked. It was why I, and many others went to these things.

I went in and saw a few people but then decided this was dumb and started to leave.

"Can I get my cards back?" I asked the older grey haired female security guard who worked for the venue, not the convention.

"Oh sure honey, here you go." She handed them to me in a plastic bag. I began to head out.

"Oh, that's the way in, honey. You have to go back out the other way." She said then went back to her work.

"Wait, I have to go back in then go back out?" I asked.

She nodded and smiled sweetly.

I pocketed my business cards and walked right back in. I threw those cards around like I was dropping hundreds at a strip club. Got a lot of work that day.

Back to Sally. I had seen Sally's work. She was a tiny young girl, early twenties, but she looked 16. She did many 'first time' lesbian scenes for companies. She was always the super shy one. The cute cheerleader or college study partner. She was preyed on by friends, step moms, teachers. Always sweet and pretty. I thought she was adorable.

Then, one day, I was editing for The Grind. The Grind is primarily a black company. They showcase large black men and small white women. The image came onto my screen and there was sweet Sally in a tank top and tiny skirt dancing by the pool. She pouted for the camera and tugged at her white cotton panties. I started to panic.

Next in the scene, Sally strolled into the house, stopping in the living room near a large white leather couch. Then two very large black men walked in and started taking her clothes off. Two. Huge. Men. The kind of men that bench press school buses for fun. The things they did to that girl still make me shudder. It was all consensual and no one was forced to do anything! This is simply MY opinion here! It was just SO shocking to see this sweet girl get railed and DPd by two black men the size of rhinos.

When I saw her at the trade show, I told her the story of how I was just taken aback. Okay, I grabbed her shoulders and said:

"Don't you ever do that to me again!" I laughed and so did she.

"I know." She laughed. "Some producers don't like when I do those scenes but I get paid so much more." She said with a sweet smile. "And I really like it."

I did some editing for her and she paid me very well and on time.

My work for The Grind was semi-steady for over six years and I got paid on time. There is only one thing that still makes me shake my head about that place. The owner could not handle technology.

I always had to drive to his offices for everything. He moved three times to smaller and smaller spaces to cut costs (and my price dropped as well with each move or rather was dropped for me) and I would drive to the new space to either pick up a hard drive or a check. With other directors, the minute the technology was available, I would upload video screeners for them to watch. With the owner of The Grind, I would have to burn a DVD and deliver it.

"See, I sit with my nighttime cocktail at my laptop and make notes." He explained one day.

Also, very late in the game he said: "Maybe I'll try to redo the website for revenue." This was at a time when many large Canadian companies had already swooped in and decimated most of the smaller companies. I had so many ideas to revitalize The Grind. He never did trade shows or events. He had launched the very successful careers of several black male performers and all were on board to help. The owner just shook his head and smiled.

"I got this." He would say. And laugh. He had a great laugh. He could talk your ear off though. He was into fitness and was often in bike shorts with a high end ten speed leaning on the wall in his office. He never could figure out the computer. He usually hand wrote my checks.

I am still waiting for the place to go under. But, I still have a stack of blank DVDs at the ready for when he calls. I will always take care of the owner of The Grind because he always did right by me.

I worked with Flame Movies for awhile. Their offices were originally in the valley like any good respectable porn company but then they moved way out past Magic Mountain, a large theme park, to an industrial park off the 5 freeway. Took an hour to get there.

I tried for a long time to be put on staff there but for some reason, it never happened. I edited a few things for them and as usual, things went well for a while. I can remember being invited up to their offices for their monthly birthday party like I was part of the family. Made me feel special.

I pitched my idea to direct to the owner many times. I had scripts, budgets worked out, and everything ready to go. Pitched to the head of sales too. He was a great salesman and always seemed genuinely interested. Never happened. But I wasn't angry about it. The place felt good. Felt like a porn company that knew it was a porn company and wasn't playing at being Warner Bros. I had many talks with him about directing and editing and ideas I had. He came from a finance background and had built the place from the ground up and knew what he was doing.

They hired D.Reck to direct for them. Out of the blue, D.Reck called me to edit for him. Since he knew me from Supreme and liked my work, this was going to be good. Remember what I said about things always start off okay? Yeah, this is one of those too. We agreed on price (low balled to death but that was the current climate) and I said yes. I always liked what he shot and he was a director on the rise. I wanted another nomination. I was ready.

Quick side bar: when I say 'low balled' here is what I mean. When I first began freelance, I could command up to $4,000 to $5,000 per feature. That included all the 'versions' (hardcore for dvd, the version they show on cable tv late at night, international edit, trailers), music and effects. To do the EXACT same work after the internet tore porn apart, was paid $2000 or less. Often less. Usually $1,500.

D.Reck and I worked together well. I was also in the middle of dealing with that family member (who eventually passed) being horribly ill. It was extremely stressful. He didn't understand that. I got no sympathy. I didn't expect special treatment but a pat on the head might have been nice. In porn, if you want sympathy, it's in the dictionary between shit and syphilis. When this family member did pass, one of my clients said: 'well thank god that's over'.

He handed me a movie he was sure was going to be a throw away. It was about a young girl discovering sex and bondage with the neighbors next door. Kinky but overall, shot well and acted well. Three cameras, I might add. Which, I happen to think are totally unnecessary. But, that is only my opinion and this is my book so … suck it.

When I handed in the movie and trailer, I walked to the warehouse with the salesman while D.Reck looked at it. I was just catching up with the salesman (he didn't own the place yet) and talking some shop when I heard my name shouted from the offices. We turned and I saw D.Reck's eyes and mouth wide as he barreled towards me.

"What? What is it?" I asked, already panicking and working up an apology.

"This is amazing. That trailer is amazing. This movie is really going to be something." He said with a smile and dragged me to his desk for a few tweaks. I was thrilled!

The movie was nominated for several awards and things were working out well. He kept me on his rotation of editors and I made that hour long drive sometimes twice a week to his offices.

Did I mention the driving I did for my clients yet? I live outside of The Valley so taking the 118 into the The Valley was a usual occurrence for me. I would plan to try and see all my clients in one trip because it was 40 minutes out or more and 40 or more back. I would get gas out there, do some shopping, stop at the AVN Offices to see friends and of course, deliver and pick up hard drives. I always dropped everything for my clients if they needed me to drive out to them - day or night. 7am or 11pm, I was driving. Got through a lot of audio books.

Then things with D.Reck got… weird. I would drive a screener out to him and he would be all smiles and couldn't wait to see it, he would call later with notes.

I would leave happy, this was all good.

Here is how this would go when he called:

beep Hey Sonny is D.Reck. Screener looks good, just a few adjustments mostly color and stuff. Easy stuff. I will call after my kid goes to bed. (He had a 4 year old)

Four hours later

beep Hey Sonny is D.Reck. Juss a few.. Um... these are easy... Really lookssss good... Call ya back.

Three hours later

beep Hey... oh my gawd... I'm.. this is... Wow, you ... do you even know what I was… Tryn to ... wo... This is gonna take a lot of work… (these words would be rather slurred).

The drunker he got, the worse the calls would get. Also, the worse it got, the more everything was my fault.

For one feature, I insisted on getting paid on a certain day as I was planning to try to go on a vacation. Oh vacations? I didn't take them. Ever. Not in ten years. This one was because a friend was visiting out of town and we had planned a wine tour. When I say she was from out of town, she was from Austria. Another country. This was more than worth taking a vacation for.

"Just gotta have the QC done." He said.

"Okay. If the QC is done in time, then I can fix the feature and we are good. If not, I can do it the minute I get back but I do need that check, okay?" I offered.

"Oh okay. That sounds fine. When you get back will work. Still way before the deadline." He said, actually smiling.

Then his QC got held up because the person was finding a lot of mistakes. Another sidebar: this person ultimately got me fired and when I did look for the 'mistakes' they were from the camera, approved by D.Reck and nothing I could fix. D.Reck wanted weird things in for a certain 'look'. So I left them in. Therefore, I was in the wrong.

"Hey, D.Reck, I'm heading out to my trip. Can I get that check?"

"The QC isn't done." He said. "You have to come to my set if you want it. I'm filming today."

"I can make the changes the minute I get back, like I said. Only going for a long weekend."

"Oh okay, that's okay then. Come on out." He said, in a good mood.

Then we drove the hour and 15 minutes to a very remote house off the beaten path. D.Reck made someone get the checkbook and wrote the check out on the hood of his car.

"You know this isn't right. I don't pay for something until it's done." He complained. I tried to remind him of the deal we had but he wasn't having it. Neither was the whiskey on his breath that nearly flattened me.

I got the check and left quickly.

Later that night, the slurred voicemail came.

beep "How dare you! I don't pay no one.. Like that… that's just… (long pause) that's just not right and you're kind of a bitch for stealing from me."

The random texts with the same line of dialogue followed.

I was done. Needed the money, but his drinking was insane.

I really should have seen it coming. When I saw D.Reck at the Flames booth at AVN before he hired me, he was SO hammered he could barely stand. His eyes were at half mast and he couldn't string an entire sentence together.

So, that was that. Oh and the last movies I did for him? All were nominated for AVN awards and awards from other publications. Thank you.

I tried to work with another large East Coast company for years and just could not get onto their roster. I interviewed, met with people. They loved me and were happy to see me at all the events.

I managed to pin down the head of post production (female) after AVN in Vegas. We met at a diner in the Valley for breakfast. I came armed with my scripts and scene breakdowns and budgets. I was ready to direct!

She handed me an editing job. I was slightly crushed.

The guy I was to work with was simply looking for someone new. I Skyped with the guy and all went very well! He was older and looked like a Good Old Boy. Baseball hat, greying hair, thick build. The kind of guy you got to rotate your tires and he knew your mama and would give you a good deal and when that was done he'd be at your house having fried chicken. We had both been in the industry a long time and spoke the same language. I had very high hopes this was going to be a great relationship.

I did the edit and sent it in for approval. I was happy with it. It looked good, was shot well, audio was great.

"The director hates it." I was told. Cold bucket of water over my head again.

The director was also the cameraman and he has this… thing he does. Every director has their trademark 'thing' they do. He shoots softcore through glass. Lamps, vases, wine glasses, whatever will blur the image enough to pass for softcore footage. I liked the effect and used it here and there. Some of these shots were two minutes or more.

"I shoot like that for a reason. I want it all used!" He screamed. I also noticed in the behind the scenes that he sat for most of the shoot. While filming. The camera was on a small set of tracks that went back and forth and he would place items in front of the camera for his swanky effect.

He was mad I didn't use the entire two minutes. Every time. Every shot. He called and emailed berating me worse and worse with every revision of this precious fuck film. I was in shock he wanted it to look the way he did but I did what he wanted and used the whole shot. He said that verbatim in the emails. Then he said:

"Don't use the WHOLE shot!" He yelled. I hung up and cried, as usual. I had been kicked in the head again.

I didn't work for him again.

I want to add another fringe director at this point to show the other side of the scale. I was not often stiffed and in over 27 years, it only happened twice. Once by a mainstream person (a lousy $75 bucks but I never saw it) and this fringe guy. He still owes me close to $2,000.

Like I said before, in freelance in adult, post-production rarely signs anything. It's an understanding and a handshake and usually, it works out just fine.

We met at a trade show and I remember being in his home to get one of the titles to edit. The place was huge but looked like he was flopping in it. The desks were strewn with flyers and papers and things were generally chaotic. His first movie with me was a baseball movie parody.

Editing for Fringe Director was okay. Not a lot of changes and he trusted my judgement. However, he was on his own and using his own money. He did pay me on time for a while but when things started to slow, so did the checks. I kept editing for him out of loyalty and should have walked away much sooner.

Eventually, he just stopped calling. I kept calling and emailing for my last checks. He moved out of state and I never heard from him again.

Until 2016.

AVN was having a party showing off their new offices. There was an open bar, food and music. Free food and free booze? The whole industry showed up. It was very cool and the place was packed. I was waiting at the bar when I hooked up with another editor friend who asked if I knew how to author DVDs. I said I did.

"Cool! The director is here!" He yelled in my ear over the pounding music.

He led me to the line waiting at the bar and Fringe turned to look at me, his eyes wide.

"Oh my god! You!" He smiled and hugged me.

"Yes me, the one you owe $2,000," I said smiling.

"No! Can't be!" He said in genuine shock. "I paid everybody."

"You forgot one," I said as I ordered my drink.

Yet, like an idiot, I agreed to work with him. I was out of work at the time and completely desperate.

He was all excited and getting back into making features. First, he wanted promos cut for the AVN show. He tells me this after my editor friend has walked away.

"I don't really like his work. I was gonna fire him anyway. Now I have you!" He beamed.

Red flags waving like I was living in a hurricane in China, yet I smiled and said yes.

He paid me once and it was $50. For one promo. He was driving Uber to pay his bills and pay for this movie. He wanted the second promo edited the same as the first. Until I asked for money. He didn't like the edit.

"Make it like the first one." He whined.

"I did. They are practically identical." I said.

"No, it's not… see… " And he proceeded to give me points in the edit.

"It's the same timeline. I just copied it and added the different girls." I explained.

"No. No, you didn't." He said flat.

But. I had. He never paid me and I never heard from him again That makes the total $2050.

CHAPTER ELEVEN

Next on my roster was Cynthia Devine. Tod knew she had been looking for an editor and he made sure she and I met. It was at Exxotica in Los Angeles when Exxotica was in Los Angeles briefly. I liked her. She was petite with big boobs and platinum hair. Plus, I got a call from another director who I also had known at Supreme.

"Are you available?" He called, slightly panicked.

"Yes I - "

"Good, get down here now." He said and hung up, texting me a downtown address. I arrived as the shoot was going on. Cynthia caught my eye and waved enthusiastically, smiling, from the set. It looked like a locker room. She was stuffed in a cheerleading outfit. Her signature platinum hair glaring in the lights.

She called me later and asked me out to lunch. We ate at a vegan/vegetarian place where the food tasted like cardboard and the walls were all pea soup green. She was sort of a health food/foodie except when there were In and Out burgers around. She made me an offer of an annual salary, paid monthly, and I agreed. It was going to be a lot of work but I was excited for the steady money. I would do whatever she wanted. Her last editor was her ex. That's a mess for another time.

Also, her demeanor at the time made you want to support her no matter what. She looked like a Barbie blow-up doll but you wanted to protect her even though she didn't need it. She had started the company in her bedroom. She had a website and DVD sales and it was all going up and up. I liked being a part of if. I had edited scenes and a feature or two but I saved one of her movies which is what sold her on me.

The set I was on was to be a movie called 'Pom Poms'. She spent the movie busting out of a too-small cheerleader's outfit. She was in the breakup process with her soon-to-be ex but he was currently the star of the movie. Also, he was still handling the website and her other movies. When the footage from the camera cards was being transferred to the hard drives, someone removed the connecting cord too soon and corrupted some of the footage. Cynthia handed me the drive with wide pleading blue eyes.

"If you can save this, I will totally love you." She said and went on about how she didn't have money to do a reshoot and what a disaster this was.

"I got this. Don't worry." I assured her but had no idea what to do.

Once I got the drive home and found the issue, I was able to save 97% of the feature. She was thrilled she didn't lose the whole thing! Just a line of dialogue or two that I was able to mask with editing. The process took a while as I had to repair the feature clip by clip but it still was in on time. I was awesome and she told me so.

In the beginning, it was great. (like always). I learned their system and put up four or five scenes a week complete with trailers. Cynthia was very hands-on and watched over every cut I did for a while. Since she was handling everything and this was her company, she was extremely mico-managy. Then she also complained about having to watch things, which was her own choice, then she stopped cold. Director's love making money and maybe they like the shooting. But once they are done, they never want to see it again. Once they've been paid, they are out. Or, they are waiting to get paid, and having to watch even one version is a pain in the ass. They just want it done to get the check. I've dealt with this a hundred times.

"I shouldn't have to watch everything!" She said to no one as she complained to the floor. She never looked at you or even up when she was saying something that might upset someone. It was an odd coping mechanism. She spread herself very thin. When there was a mistake on something, she smacked with one hand and pet me with the other. It was very weird but I made sure I was more careful, not that it really mattered. Being that I was new to their system and still learning was not an excuse, it seems. Or, maybe she didn't tell me 100% of the job, maybe 75% but I was supposed to just know 100%. It was like that.

"You know this is all I do. This is everything." She would say over the phone or sometimes in an email.

"I know and I am so sorry. I didn't know the deadlines. I don't have them yet." I would explain.

"Oh, but you should just know. It's common sense." She would say as if reading her mind was part of the job. Then she would rattle off the entire upload schedule which she had been working with for years and I wasn't given the information yet. I would scribble in a notebook like a fiend and pray. Eventually, I just worked with her business partner/money man. He was much more reasonable. Then again, he had small children and knew how to handle tantrums.

When her website was bought by Godzilla (THE largest of the Canadian companies), things went smoother. As Cynthia had me on the 'you are a screw up' bandwagon, Godzilla sent me a bottle of champagne and thanked me for the great job I was doing. So, I didn't suck after all and I had Pierre Jouet as proof. Stepping outside of an abusive relationship like that makes you see the sun. It was refreshing and gave me confidence that Cynthia made sure to crush often.

So, the ex. He was always real with me. He wasn't always 'on' and being a 'porn star'. He was always honest. He handed over all the hard drives when I took over and said if I needed any help to just ask. I think he respected me because I was an older female and unfuckable. Probably his mom's age. I recently reconnected with him and we realized we have a pretty good friendship. We are going to dish dirt soon, just for fun.

Along with the editing, he would sometimes shoot BTS, Behind The Scenes, of video shoots. I offered to take over that job. I always wanted to film and Cynthia said yes. She was shocked I had even offered. I had my own little HD camera and was excited! Of course, I would do the first one for free then we would talk money later. This is what I told her and she agreed. I shot on every set for every scene and she never paid me an extra dime. My fault, I suppose, right? Oh, and that added to my editing as well since I shot it and edited it. I became the BTS Bitch (yes, I got that from Kelly Kapoor from The Office TV show). She added the BTS clips to the upload schedule and it was more footage for her to make money from and more work for me. I was an idiot, have I mentioned that?

The only cool thing to happen from that was I was recognized for my voice. See, the BTS clips got very popular on the website. I used my name 'Sonny' and my own voice etc. I had fun with the girls and other talent as well as everyone on set! I wasn't derogatory and always tried to make the girls laugh or be at ease. The usual BTS is often shot by a production assistant or some other low-level male on set. He often takes the girl into a room, alone, and within five minutes he is breathing like a 976 phone call asking about her tits and grabbing one. The girl just had to giggle and take it. I never once grabbed a girl. Cynthia always claimed she was trying to be hands-off, then this would happen:

Me in the bedroom/makeup room with the girl: So, tell me something random. When did you first color your hair?

Girl: looks at her bright green locks: Oh um... when I was -

Cynthia suddenly at the door: Hey, ask about her hair. This is a rainbow-themed movie.

Girl and I stop and look at Cynthia as she munches dried seaweed.

Me: Yeah, I was.

Cynthia: Okay, I don't want you to forget that.

And she turns on her heel and leaves. Girl and I blink at each other for a few minutes and get on with the questions.

Me: Tell me about your first celebrity crush.

Cynthia - screaming from another room: Ask the celebrity question!

This was her *not* micromanaging.

At a dive bar one night. Cynthia was hosting an amateur stripper contest. I showed up and said hi, hugging her and her new man, Moses.

"Oh my god, I know that voice!" An Australian-accented female voice said behind me. She was tall with dark hair, covered in tattoos, and very pretty. "You're Sonny!" She said and hugged me tight.

She was a singer/rapper from Australia who was in town and loved Cynthia's work but seemed she loved mine too! It was great to be noticed. We still stay in touch. Thank you, Facebook!

On the wrong end of that BTS, I shot a birthday party at her house/set. I shot everything. I could usually get the girls to make out or something and it would be extra footage for the site and no one seemed to mind. But this was a party, not a regular shoot.

"Go get the stuff in the bedroom," Cynthia whispered, shoving the camera in my hand and sending me on my way. When I got to the bedroom, a full-on five-person orgy was happening. So, I shot. I had to follow a leg here and an arm there to get to the person. It was like Twister with no board. I sort of hoped she might let me do camera now and then so I was anxious to show off my chops. When she did live sex stuff on the web, I did shoot that for her because I did it for free and it was free footage for the website. I wasn't smart. I was loyal.

The orgy footage was broken into multiple clips and put on the website. Everyone sort of did stuff for Cynthia. Girls lowered their prices. I did things for free. We all did. When a male performer got upset about some of the orgy footage making it out into the world, I didn't get it. Then I did. He basically did a free scene. He was there to celebrate a friend's birthday, not perform. I really liked this guy personally. We met up randomly at the grocery store once and hugged it out. He knew I was only taking orders. When he goes live on Instagram, I always jump into the chat.

I banged my head against a lot of walls in this industry. Usually happens when I am trying to make friends. Once I wanted to be friends with everyone's favorite drunk comic cameraman, Lincoln. I mention him here because this is where I met him, working for Cynthia.

He always made me happy when I walked onto the set.

"Sunshine!" He would exclaim if he wasn't shooting.

"Lincoln, my love, how goes it?" I would answer.

"Oh, ya know. Not drunk enough and still wanting to kill myself daily." He laughed. "Hide the knives and drain cleaner! I got porn to shoot!"

He and I had a lot of things in common. We knew Porn's place in this world and making high-end stuff was nice and all but the basic gonzo naked chick movies were the real bread and butter. When things had been good, he had made a lot of money and now the internet had happened and he was selling his house. If you think my price fell, the same thing happened to people like him. When I started with Cynthia, Linc had a two-person crew with him: Fred (impossibly old man, lighting) and Barney (cute younger kid, PA, and grip). He had cute songs made up about both of them and we would all join in and laugh. Linc was the life of the party and his crew was loyal. By the end of things, it was just Linc. Cynthia could not afford Fred or Barney. Her new man, Moses, took over both of those jobs for free.

Linc and I sat together only a handful of times on the set when we could really talk. We talked the closest when Robin Williams died as we had also both been stand-up comedians in a former life. We talked about when things were going wrong with his stepson. When he lost his house, I was a good shoulder. I liked talking to him. It was nice to have someone that understood what I did as he edited things he shot for other companies as well.

For a while, I could count on him. If I just needed to talk, I could text and if he could, he would text back. If I needed technical advice, he was there and always helpful. But, one didn't get too close to Linc. He made sure of it. It was personal, it was his self-preservation.

If we were talking closely, Manzie, the guy who did the stills for the website and box covers, would walk in and break things up. Usually ignoring the fact that I was there completely. Like I was not even in the room. Manzie was a tall Hispanic guy in his early 30s, bald and slender with an accent. I would join Linc wherever he had set up his laptop, setting my camera down and taking advantage of the quiet time. I would ask about his family and how he was doing. It usually went like this:

Me to Linc: *I have the same issue with that director. If you want to talk later?*

Linc would lift his eyes from the screen and connect with me for a brief moment. His eyes were clear and honest.

Linc: *You know, I'd like that. We can -*

Manzie: *brushing past me like I was a coat hanging on a chair* *Yo, Linc. Look at the titties on this one!* *shoving the view screen of his camera in Linc's face*

Linc *Whoa! Flotation devices!*

Conversation with me - over. Linc's eyes, shadowed and closed off.

Cynthia filmed in her home. It was at the end of a long driveway therefore out of the way. Even though it was in the middle of The Valley. I would show up with my purse, laptop and hard drive, and my stitch work. Usually embroidery. I would set up the laptop to transfer footage as it was shot to be ready to take it home at the end of the shoot. I would also transfer BTS footage as I shot it. Moses would make food, and we ate, shot, and drank (not drunk drink, but down a shot here and there because it was always a party atmosphere).

Cynthia would fly in a girl to shoot each month. I sometimes would pick them up from the LAX airport shuttle in the Valley and bring them to the house. Often it was a brand-new girl. I never had a description but they were never hard to pick out; a Barbie doll dressed like a drag queen or a young girl in shoes too high and one suitcase too big. A stand out in Wisconsin but is the norm here. I will say they were all really sweet.

Being thrown into this environment, they often gravitated toward me. I was close to their mom's age and overweight, I was safe and non-threatening. If the actual sex scene wasn't being shot, I would walk around with my camera and shoot BTS. I would conduct interviews and shoot random things around the house. While the scene was being shot, I would be on the couch or in whatever room wasn't being used. I would be with the rest of the girls who were waiting to shoot; their faces buried in the phones. I would pull out a pillowcase I was stitching something onto: butterflies, flowers, dancing Grateful Dead bears. I did a lot of stitch work while hardcore anal sex was only a thin wall away.

Once, I brought a large tablecloth I was working on and a male performer slowly slid up to me.

"Hey... embroidery?" He asked. He was very young and as bright as a flashlight bulb.

"Yeah, a tablecloth," I said. He smiled wide.

"I knew it. My mom does that!" He said and sat, asking questions and watching me. He knew the whole process and was very proud of that fact. He waited on me for the rest of the shoot. He filled my tea, and got me food, did I need anything? Then he would go off and plow some too-thin young girl on camera. Often calling her a bitch. Often slapping her. Then, he would wave happily to me as he passed, naked and sweating, on the way to the shower. Ah, such a sweet child.

Cynthia got used to me. She often called from out of town to have me help her out with random things. She gave me the keys to her house.

"I'm going to be late, can you feed my cat?"

I would drive the half hour to her apartment, feed the cat, play with her a bit, and then drive back home. I did that often. That's the kind of thing I did for my clients.

When she was asked to be a part of a Fall Erotic Film Festival in Denver, she asked me to go with her. I was shocked and flattered. My partner said to go, it would be good for my relationship with Cynthia and I agreed. I did the film festival edit of one of her films; it was a Hallmark movie parody. Very funny, as usual, with hard-core anal sex. Like ya do. We flew to Denver and were driven around the city in a town car by a man who thought he was shooting a chase scene. I was terrified. Cynthia's face was glued to her phone. At the festival, she was greeted like a star, which she is. We watched the festival entries and I started to get very scared. These were erotic and hers had HARD core anal sex. She had approved the cut! I was still mortified as the rowdy crowd fell dead silent as Cynthia's ass filled the art house screen with a large penis in it. This went on for what felt like days. I tried to disappear into the seat. When I apologized over and over again later, she just shrugged. But, this was to be our one and only trip together.

"I approved it. It's whatever." She said, then went back to her phone, tugging on a lock of her hair. She always did that with her bleached blonde extensions. Always. My embarrassment or anything uncomfortable was dismissed.

We went out to dinner with people she knew afterward and I might as well have gone to the hotel. I was ignored. I looked like the damn chaperone around the truly hip club kids dressed head to toe in pink. They were awesome, don't get me wrong. I tried to talk to them, I did my best. But it was clear, I was not part of the Cool Kids. I still don't know why she invited me. Maybe she was trying to be pals? I do not know. I knew we were 'friends' to a point and we could talk to each other but this trip seemed strained from the get-go. Even in the hotel room, she barely talked to me. To be fair, we had nothing in common.

Flash forward to another movie and another crisis. The movie revolved around girls at a bar, like Coyote Ugly. She had an actual set and stage and mock bar set up complete with bottles. It looked fairly authentic. With all that attention to detail, recorded sound would have been nice. Decent sound. Not sound I had to invent from another camera and try to make it match. For some reason, the boom mic wasn't plugged in for the entire feature. Two different cameras shot the movie and both with different frame rates. Real high-end end here. The only audio I had drifted every few seconds. No, Lincoln was not on this shoot. He would have caught that.

In the middle of this fiasco, the ill family member fell very ill and was admitted to the hospital where he stayed for two months. It was so serious that my partner's sister and husband flew out from the east coast. Her sister was a lawyer and she was setting up any Power of Attorney paperwork etc. It was getting dire.

As we were ready to go to the hospital, my phone rang. I saw it was Cynthia.

"Hey, how is the movie coming along?" She asked.

"Good, I will get to it tonight."

"Oh but it's due soon!" She said starting to panic. I could almost hear the hair tugging.

"Yes, I know. I will work on it tonight. We are about to go to the hospital." I explained. She knew all about the ill family member.

She sighed so heavily I swore I caught the scent of her pink lip gloss through the phone.

"You know, I need you on this. This is due and I know you have family stuff but I am paying you." She said with her dry laugh that was supposed to lighten the mood. I started to cry but didn't let her know.

I took my partner and her sister to the hospital then dropped them off, racing back home to work on the movie. This went on the whole time the sister was in town.

Okay, I know I'm supposed to be looking for the funny in my little porn world. Sometimes, it just wasn't. I wish it was all blowjobs and fake boobs. Okay, no I don't. Moving on.

I worked with Cynthia for four years. I watched her shoot go from locations in downtown LA to her house only. I actually hated the downtown shoots. The areas were so sketchy I was always secretly relieved when my car would still be where I parked it when the shoot was over. I made deals with all sorts of deities all the way down the dark street, my finger on the electronic key opener. I would press it and nearly cheer when the familiar beep-beep would happen and I would hear the doors unlock. At her place, I knew the area and I felt safe. Downtown would be some random brick loft space full of grit and dirt and I would want to come home and burn my clothes. She had one guy doing stills in a particular downtown location that she used to use a lot when I first started with her. She wanted me to get as much BTS footage as possible so I would often film the photo shoots. Content was content at any price and could be sold.

This guy hated it. He lived in this warehouse space and he was sort of eccentric. Or, just an asshole, who knows. But when I filmed behind him, he would not look at me. More on this later.

When I told Cynthia I wanted the company to have an editing award she laughed. Literally.

"We don't get awards for editing." She said, twirling her hair. Her eyes were glued to her phone as I was dismissed as usual. I was going to prove her wrong.

One of my favorite movies I did for her was a Meet-Cute-style murder mystery parody.

It had been a while since I'd seen a too-sweet Hallmark movie so I watched a few to get the vibe. Her long-time friend, Lee Dorsey, was going to play the lead. This was pretty much his baby. He wanted to do a straight movie of the week murder mystery film but Cynthia's trademark was Barbie-like comedies. All comedies. It was all she ever did. They butted heads over how to handle it and in the end, both got directing credits. Even though they had been friends for years, she complained in my ear about how this was her company and that she was putting up most of the money, and that it should be only her name on things. She would do this coiled into a chair, twirling her hair, and balancing her phone on her massive boob job. It was beginning to feel like the Empire (TV show) drinking game. Whenever she said 'company', you took a shot. She and Lee went way way back and he was part of her starting the company (drink here) back in the day. The fun part was the editing!

I got to edit this mystery romp movie with action sequences and cheesy graphics, sound effects, and video effects. The only editing downside was the orgy at the end. Cynthia and a male performer were in the same scene. The problem was, that Cynthia was playing this performer's mother and this movie was going through Moralle. Everything had to be top drawer. I did a version for Moralle and DVD release and a version for the website. Two versions had to have her and this other performer not having sex or even touching. She had forgotten that most of the movie had this guy calling her Mom. One version has the scene completely cut out.

I even researched how to duplicate the opening credits from the original movie and found a download with the correct font and effects. I was very proud.

Cynthia may have been right about her company (drink) not winning any editing awards, BUT I did get her company its first editing nomination.

There was one movie before this mystery parody. It was a 60's beach movie/cheesy horror flick parody. This one was indeed shot for comedy and it was funny! It was also… sticky. Also… kinda gross. Let me explain.

First off, most of her movies were shot in that downtown warehouse space. The stills guy she used (and he lived there, remember) was an odd duck, which is the best way I can put that. Anti-social and gruff. He hated it when I filmed the photo shoots. The video I shot of the girl posing for stills was added as extra behind-the-scenes for the website. Stills were used for either the box or for promotions.

Everyone was hanging out, like usual, while the stills got taken. People were not loud or partying but the place was a warehouse and had a massive echo. I grabbed the video camera and slipped in behind the guy as he shot and made sure I was out of his way. I was pressed against the back wall and tried to make myself as small as possible. I was easily more than ten feet away from him. After a few clicks, he froze. He huffed out a huge breath, all but slammed the camera down, and stormed off the set without a word. I went to Cynthia and told her what had happened but my voice was hushed and I was shaking a little. She found him pouting in his very large bedroom. He said we were all being too loud and he didn't want me near the shoot.

Yea, he was an odd duck. So we all had to whisper and stay out of his way while he shot. But that meant less footage for the website.

Sets were built for this movie rather than just adding new pillows to existing furniture. We were making a parody of this movie so we needed a specific set. In this case, a beach house with a bedroom and a hallway. Since this was a slasher film, there was going to be a lot of fake blood. A lot. One more time for the cheap seats: A LOT.

One of her stars, Alena, was in a bad blonde curly wig and ready to be 'hacked up'. She was a sweet girl and a good actress. Also, helped that her husband was Cynthia's business partner and they had two kids. She also gave Cynthia a price cut.

The blood pack was set and it had to spurt from her neck when the killer slashed her throat. Getting the contraption to go up her shirt to her throat took time. Things were finally set up and off it went! It was everywhere! Kayro syrup and red dye stuck to every surface for weeks after the shoot. Since the stills guy was kind of an ass, it made me smile inside, just a little.

The shoot there ran like usual otherwise. However, Cynthia and Lee Dorsey wanted to do more. Lee was the other mind behind this movie as well. All Cynthia did was try and grab credit for as much as she could. She somehow was not up for the collaborative effort. Unless it was Lee trying to grab too much? Either way, it was just as awkward as the other one.

For this movie, there was a night shoot featuring an exterior at a location by a lake. A false front was built that actors could run in and out of. It was a pretty big shoot for a Cynthia feature. There was a grip truck and make-up people and a director-type person who was very eager to make this all go well. Cynthia did all the directing after this, she never collaborated again. The 'director' on this one was someone she had worked with before for another mainstream rom-com thing, therefore, her pal. To get to the set, it was an hour-long drive that ended with a dirt road, a one-lane dirt road so lord help you if anyone came the other way. It was also the hottest night on record that year. Close to 95 degrees at 4 am even by the water.

In the original movie, a girl runs into the water and the killer seaweed grabs her from the edge of the water and seemingly tear her apart. Or have sex with her. In this one, she was going to have sex with a killer octopus. Hey, porno movie here. Alena ran from the house and onto the beach to the edge of the water in the dark. When the seaweed caught her, some was some real seaweed but the octopus was made of moldable plastic, and one shorter tentacle was made with a type of plastic that could be... well.. inserted. She was going to be fucked by an octopus. Welcome to porn and Cynthia's company (insert drink here. I said 'company' on purpose to get that drink, you are welcome!)

There was one young mainstream makeup girl on the set that night that I had not seen before. She was petite and Asian and sort of shy and had helped make the octopus. She had no idea what she had gotten herself into. I had been on sets long enough that to be around naked bodies having sex wasn't new to me. Still weird, but not new. We all had to pitch in and grab some seaweed and pretend to be clawing at Alena's naked body while the tentacle had its way with her. This went on for about ten minutes. I watched the girls' bunch of now-dried seaweed next to me go slower and slower and back away. When 'cut' was called, she dropped her seaweed and all but ran. I followed her. She was shaking and pale.

"Hey, it's okay," I said softly and put my arm around her.

"Just... I dunno... Not something I'm used to seeing I guess." She said softly and huddled into me. I mean we were inches away from a writhing naked female being fucked by a plastic tentacle (that this girl had helped make) rather enthusiastically by a director who did not know his way around the female anatomy. I got it.

I sat with her in the makeup area and just kept her calm. I watched Cynthia roll her eyes at us and all but laugh with the others as the shoot went on.

Alena was on the sand on a moving blanket while this was going on and the guy with the tentacle/dildo was very into this. He went way too hard on her and she had to stop things a few times. Then, the ants started to take over when they caught the scent of strawberry lube. The director got it free at some convention. The scene ended quickly but still got a nomination for Most Outrageous Sex Scene. Ya think?

The movie was done but we needed an opening sequence. I had watched parts of the feature and was left to my own devices. Since I lived up in the mountains, I set my camera on the dashboard of my car and simply drove home. After tweaking the footage a bit, It looked perfect and all but matched the original film.

While working for Cynthia, I still had other freelance clients. She knew this and had no problem. Sometimes she even recommended me to other people. But she always said:

"But you can't leave me okay? You've got a job for life!"

More on that later.

CHAPTER TWELVE

What I did for my clients. Everything.

I would plan my trips to see my clients in groups. Drop off a hard drive here. Pick up a check here. See a potential new director here. Get lunch. Go home.

This happened about three times a week. I listened to a lot of audiobooks and eventually could do the drive blindfolded. I would load up the snacks and water and fill the tank in Porn Valley. Gas prices were better.

Of course, I am making this sound easy but it was really like herding cats. I would do my best to group at least three directors on one trip. Then the text or email would come in to change the day. Usually, the day change came from one who owed me a check.

By the end of all my negotiations, it would only be one stop. Hence the drive out three times a week. Change the day? Sure. Meet you on the set instead of the office? Sure. Wash your car when I get there? Anything you say.

I did anything, and everything, to please the client.

Eventually, I took my partner with me and we would make a day of it. Client, then lunch and shopping. We would plan the week around the trip. So when the client would cancel, it would upend the whole day we had planned. But, I am lucky to have a very understanding partner and we would just shift things around. Yes, it was highly annoying but... money. Ya know? Anything for the client.

When my father was visiting from Connecticut, I took him on one of my Valley jaunts. He had been a traveling salesman of sorts and I hoped he would be proud of the effort I put in to please a client. We went to see four different clients and then grabbed lunch. When we got home, he fell asleep on the couch right after he praised me for the effort I made to make my clients happy. I was overjoyed.

Caleb Rosebanks was a former performer at Moralle. He had graduated to director and had become a staple at the company. I had admired his comedic work for years and first discovered him when I was at Porn Town. I was in awe! He was funny, tall, and handsome. He had aged very well and was now distinguished. I remember fumbling over my words when I met him at Moralle.

Dropping off something for Cynthia, he walked in to talk to the post supervisor and I was dumbstruck. I was looking up at him because he was so tall. I shook his hand, made sure he had my card, and after he left told the post supervisor how much I would love to work with him.

It finally happened. Here is the second time I met Caleb.

It was at the XRCO Awards in Hollywood. I was a guest of an older performer from back in the day and she was getting a lifetime achievement award. I had done some work for her but she was pretty much done with the industry. I sat in the VIP section, alone, and watched the show. I said hi to some folks, as usual, had a drink or two, and mingled. By this time, everyone here knew who I was or had my card so networking wasn't needed. Only so many times you can ask someone for work. It had gotten to the point where it was almost a joke. I would walk up to someone and they would automatically say:

"I don't have anything for you." Then, the laugh.

"So, buy me a drink!" Then the hug.

Eventually, I stopped asking. If they had work, they would call me.

I stayed for most of the event then headed out to get my car from the valet. While waiting with the rest of the crowd, I watched the girl who had hosted the event make her way around the waiting cars in the valet line. She was painfully thin, with short cropped bleached hair and wide brown eyes. The girl was tottering on platform high heels like a baby giraffe in a dress that was more like a sequined napkin; too short and sparkling. A male performer was holding her up. She began to yell and crouched down to take off her painful shoes. She was drunk as hell and a complete wreck.

Most of the guys in the valet line whipped out their cell phones to take pictures. I helped the guy get her to the curb. She plopped down with her huge purse and started to rummage through it. When I say huge, I mean I think I could have carried her IN it!

"She's not okay," I said. He nodded.

"I know. She drank a lot." He said in his clipped Italian accent. "I can get her home I think." He said and crouched next to her. "Honey, where do you live?" He asked.

"I lmmph vrp... Mggmg" Was her answer and she dove back into her bag up to her shoulders.

"She's one of Caleb's girls." A male voice said from the crowd. I stood up.

"Caleb?" I asked.

"Yea, Caleb Rosebanks." Another male performer said. He had his phone out and was texting. I had been unaware Caleb had started a modeling agency.

"So, where is Caleb?" I asked. I was met with shugs and lots of 'I dunno'. People were starting to drift away from the trainwreck. I grabbed the guy's arm, as I knew him from a Cynthia shoot (she even shot in his loft downtown a few times).

"Then give me his number. You got your phone out. Help me here." I said, probably a little louder than I should have but with definitely enough force. He texted me Caleb's number. I texted and got no response so I called.

"Hello?" Caleb answered.

"Caleb? It's Sonny Malone. I have one of your girls here and she needs some help. Where are you?" I asked. He took a beat to answer.

"I'm at home. I didn't go tonight. Is she okay?" He asked, genuinely concerned. I looked at the girl and she was inches from passing out.

"She's gonna get arrested for public drunkenness." The performer who gave me the number and other male voices laughed. I made a decision.

"Text me your address. I am bringing you a girl." Just then, my car pulled into the valet spot and the Italian performer gently placed her into the passenger seat. She threw up in my car in seconds.

Fun. The guys laughed more. The Italian guy helped me clean her up as best I could, I covered her with a blanket, made sure she had her purse and I drove her deep into the Valley.

That is not a euphemism. Caleb's condo was off the last exit of the 101 before you hit the other side of Mars. It took 45 minutes (from the heart of Hollywood) with no traffic. If you live in Los Angeles, you would get that.

For the record here, the next time I saw the Italian performer, he didn't even say hello to me. We talked for a long time while we tried to figure out what to do with said girl. He even hit on me! That was that. It was a one-night fling.

When I got to Caleb's, I parked out front and he met me. He was wearing a T-shirt, sweats, and slippers. We had hoped to get the girl to his place on her own power. No dice.

"You'd better park around the back, in the lot." He said and jogged around to open the gate.

I parked in the handicapped spot (I had the placard from that ill family member) and we got her to the elevator.

"Nice place," I said and he laughed.

"Oh yeah, great drunk girl drop-off spot." He smiled. "I'm thinking of adding wheelbarrow to door service."

We all but dragged the poor thing to his condo. She was tall and all arms and legs that seemed to flop around like a rag doll. We got her into bed (an air mattress in his second bedroom) and she kept throwing up. Caleb was scared to death. Once she was calmer, he grabbed a roll of paper towels and we went back to my car to clean things up.

"I am so sorry for all of this. This is so nice of you." He said as we mopped up the earlier mess.

"No trouble. I mean I wasn't going to just leave her there." I said.

"Most people would." He said softly.

Back in the apartment, the girl was sick less and starting to snore.

"Can you ... stay for a bit? Until she is.... Better?" He asked uneasily. He had gone white watching her.

We sat in the living room and talked. She was new and was in town to shoot a few scenes. Fast forward, she didn't last more than a few months. Oh no, she didn't die, she just left the business. We talked about how the business had changed over the last twenty years as his cats explored my purse. The condo was a nice two-bedroom place. The living room had been taken over by an editing station and desk since the second bedroom was for wayward up-and-coming porn stars.

Eventually, she slept.

"I don't know how I can repay you." He said as I stood to leave after over an hour had passed.

"Easy. Hire me. Or at least buy me lunch." I smiled. "I'll text you some time," I said. We hugged and I was gone. I texted that same night when I got home to make sure she was okay. He thanked me for my concern and she was fine, he hoped, and he was going to bed. Yes, I texted the next day. The girl was fine.

Three months later, I hadn't heard from him and didn't expect to. I was cleaning out my car and found the remainder of the clean paper towel roll. I snapped a picture and texted it to Caleb.

"Lunch?" I messaged. Within a half hour, he texted back.

"Yes!" He texted and I was shocked.

We met near his house one afternoon and I expected lunch. I genuinely liked the guy and if there was no work in the future, that was fine. I sort of idolized him back in the day and it was just awesome to meet someone who had been in the business as long as I was. We had a lot in common and could talk as friends.

We met and ordered, then sat and waited for our food.

"What are the odds you happen to message me this week when I am looking for a new editor?" He said.

I blinked like an owl.

"Really?" I said, the heart fluttering a little.

I started with clean-up work on his features then he handed me a whole one. We both knew how Moralle worked and I knew all the legal guidelines.

"One thing. Keep my name off of it?" I asked. I explained my past Bryan Salte history and he simply nodded.

"I am perfectly okay with that." He assured me.

"Unless it's going to be nominated, then put my name on." I joked and he laughed.

I loved working for Caleb. When I handed in my first revision, he didn't text or email, he called. Calls were usually a bad thing.

"You know, sometimes you just know when you find the right editor and today I can say, I found the right editor." He said, I was crying now for a different reason, I was being praised! "You chose all the shots I would have, the cuts are right on. It's really good." He said.

Of course, we had the same mind, we had come through the ranks the same years, the same firestorm. We matched and I was on cloud nine. Did I get it right for once?

Yes, I had. Briefly.

I was leaving town for a little while and would work on the road. Just a personal trip out of Dodge. Caleb assured me he would still, and always, hire me.

"Doesn't matter where you are, hard drives ship. I won't lose you." He said when I said goodbye.

I had done about 4 movies for him so I knew his style, obviously, but this new feature had a real Tarantino shoot-em-up feel and I wanted to show that angle. I followed the script he had written, as usual, with a different special effect for showing a flashback that I had seen in a recent mainstream movie. It was all bad.

He called me after I sent in the first revision and proceeded to lecture me on how to edit porn. It was as if we had never talked and this was my first film for him. Or rather, my first porn film ever. He belittled me and talked down to me. Talked to me like I was a child and was rather stupid for 45 minutes. He would get that tone in his voice like he was talking to a slow Burger King employee, reciting their own menu back to them and why we could have It Your Way.

Somehow I finished the feature and got paid. Personally, I was crushed. I dared to step out of his comfort zone.

Two and a half weeks later, we were back in Los Angeles.

I returned his hard drive and gave him one of mine for future projects. There would not be any. When I saw him at AVN the following year, he smiled and hugged me, and moved on in seconds. We never talked. I truly miss him. And his cats.

Zelah Gordon was a photographer I had known for a long time at Supreme and from my years in the industry. He was creative and interesting. When he got let go from Supreme suddenly, he called me. I was still working there.

"Hey, can you do me a favor?" He asked, his voice was a little shaky. I think he was stunned.

"Sure, what's up?" I asked.

"They won't give me copies of my work there. Like the movies I made. I want only one particular one. Can you grab a DVD of it for me?" He asked and gave me the title.

"Of course, I will let you know when I have it!" I said reassuringly.

I did get it and I called him and never heard back. I saw him years later when I was working for Cynthia and she had rented these cheap stages in the worst part of the Valley. Everyone in the industry shot there and it showed in the mess and neglect. Like someone hosted a party and forgot the clean-up crew. Zelah was distracted like he didn't know who I was. I said I still had the DVD and he waved me away. I did some work for that studio myself. It was hell on earth and thankfully a short gig. The people I worked for had systems from the Stone Age and refused to be compatible with newer technology. I couldn't go backward that far.

Years and years later I get a text.

Hey - do you still do freelance? - Zelah

I did a movie for him about picking up friends at red lights and how the night can take twists and turns. It was inventive but straightforward. Since he also worked in mainstream, his shots were beautiful and too good for porn. One shot, in particular, I liked and had to fight for.

"See? If I leave the shot on the driver here, he has this cool look on his face. Like he is actually acting." I said with a slight laugh.

"No, cut to the girl getting into the car," Zelah said, eyes squinted as he looked down his nose, glasses sliding off, at the screen.

So I did. She climbed in with each take with all the grace of a baby gorilla navigating a mud puddle.

"Okay, you are right. Your way is better." He said and smiled. "I will listen to you from now on!" He patted my back.

Zelah wanted more work from Moralle. He wanted to be their new powerhouse. I warned him of my past with that company but he waved it off. He loved my work and that was that. I kept my name off that first film and it got a bunch of nominations. I heard it would have gotten a Best Editing nod but no editor was listed.

When I did the second film for Zelah, he insisted my name be on it.

"Seriously, you are awesome and this is a collaborative effort." He said. I had never had a director fight for me since Frank at Porn-Town 25 years prior. So, I put my name on it. I will call that the Kiss of Death. The second film, had a few nominations but Moralle didn't push it very hard.

A year later I saw the press release for his third film with Moralle. Obviously, I didn't edit it. I warned him that putting my name on things would do this. I am sure they gave him the 'you have to work with our approved editors or else'. He chose the 'or else' and they still spanked him by not giving him anything else to direct. Except for that once-a-year crumb.

That, my friends, is porn loyalty.

For the record: I held on to that DVD he asked me to grab for him for over 10 years. I moved twice - once across the country and back - but I always kept track of it. I finally handed it to him on our last meeting at my house. THAT is my idea of porn loyalty.

I am adding someone here to show how not being in porn but knowing someone in porn can change their perception of you.

Before I worked at PornTown, I took a freelance job editing a promotional video about anti-microbial soap for hospitals. The director rented an AVID and I worked out of his home. The guy that owned that system was Mainstream Guy. He and I had crossed paths at that first edit bay since he was our technician.

"Oh, so you took my job!" He joked and smiled as he set up the AVID.

"I didn't know! So sorry!" I laughed as well. I had hung over his shoulder a lot to learn all I could about the machine and he taught me everything he could.

We stayed friends. As I moved through adult companies, It was he who told me I needed to have a 401k and find a place that would respect me. He was one of the reasons I moved to Supreme.

As time went on, he would also help troubleshoot my home system but refused to charge me. He was in my home several times and we remained good friends. Until….

His comments regarding my sex life became increasingly invasive.

"You and your partner, you watch this and get off right?" He said. He was leering and laughing but that laugh was sour.

"Well, no." I laughed as well, figuring he was kidding. I was getting uncomfortable.

Then he started to name our biological parts and how my partner could service me under the desk while I worked. This is the problem with having a friend outside of the industry. They think that since I work around sex all day I must have sex all the time. Crazy unhinged weird sex. I was just a regular person who had regular sex. Not that it is anyone's business anyway.

"But, you want to right?" He asked, his hand sliding to his crotch. The only other bad thing about this was I was living in a studio apartment so my desk was five feet from the bed. My partner was on her laptop next to me on the bed typing and trying not to punch his lights out.

"I mean, I could climb right in the middle there and you can show me all you've learned." He joked. I stood up.

"Yeah, it is super late and I have to get to this edit," I said and he stood up too.

"Oh yeah sure. It is late." He said and gathered his things and I walked him out. He hugged me too long and I shuddered. I didn't see him for a while. My choice. We don't talk much anymore and frankly, that is just fine with me.

CHAPTER THIRTEEN

I knew the end was coming with Cynthia. It was a long slow down-hill road for about a year. You know that video of the small child going down the slide but they get stuck and it takes forever for them to get down? That was me.

First, I noticed the lack of staff. Linc had cut two of his guys and Moses was running around picking up the slack. From cooking to lighting to paperwork, he did it all. Then one day, on set at another location, Cynthia sat me down.

"Here it is. I want to change things up. I want you to learn to make DVDs." She said without looking at me. "But be clear I WON'T be paying you more! That has to be clear! I won't be paying you more." She said to the carpet emphatically.

I sort of blinked at the insistence of that. "Okay," I said, stunned.

"Moses is going to take over doing the trailers." She said then finally looked at me. "That helps, right? Do one thing less but do the DVDs." She said, her eyes wide.

"Yeah, sure," I said.

"Cause, it's not that I don't like what you are doing but it's all the same and I want things to look different." She explained once again to the carpet, twirling her bracelets so hard I thought she was going to unscrew her wrist. It was the same tune all over again I had heard so many times.

Director: *I am going to shoot the exact same thing every time but you have to make it completely different every time, k?*

Me: *Oh could I have more time to do the edit then? Bigger budget for effects? Little more money to get more bells and whistles for the edit suite?*

Director: * blinks like an owl at me* *I am going to shoot the exact same thing every time but you have to make it completely different every time, k?*

Cynthia shot the same thing. All the time. Comedy stuff with cheerleaders. She didn't change what she shot but she wanted it edited differently. Yeah, it started there. Then the shoots were only at her home so the set was always the same. Shoots at other locations stopped cold. She was simply trying to save money but she never explained it like that to me. Nor did she explain what she wanted exactly. She never said what new vibe she was going for. I was a twenty-year professional and making a change like that wasn't difficult. But if you look at a blue wall and say 'paint it more blue' it kind of leaves me out of the creative process. She didn't tell me that Moses did some trailers and she liked them. And he was free.

For everything Cynthia shot, she used the same people or painfully brand-new girls. Herself and Moses were in every movie (no need to pay anyone else), Dane, a male performer (he gave them a good price and he was still up and coming), Lee (old friends so, good price), and brand new girls (cheaper for their inexperience in the industry). Also, her usual stable of girls would cut their price for her.

Then Moses started to write all the music for trailers and the scenes. I was still editing the best way I knew how and now Moses was editing the openings to give them this 'new' look. He was fried at all ends and it showed every time I saw him. His eyes were hollow and he looked exhausted. The 'new look' was pretty much 90's MTV.

"All for the head cheerleader, right?" He would say and down another shot of booze.

Once I went to Cynthia's place to pick up a hard drive but she wasn't there. It was just Moses and a friend of his. It was over 100 outside and the AC was iffy in my car.

"Can you stay for a bit? Want a beer?" He offered. I usually don't drink beer but there was something slightly pleading in his eyes and the way his hand reached for my arm.

"Sure." I smiled and dropped my purse.

He handed me an ice-cold Modelo from the fridge, opening it first. It hit my throat like that liquid sunshine everyone tells you about. The air was on in the house and the usually bustling place was quiet. No shoot. No extra girls. Just me and the two guys. We talked about editing and the biz and I started to relax. Then Moses busted out with this:

"How are you doing? How is (the ill family member)?" He asked, actually looking at me concerned. I blinked a few times then answered his question, tears rising in my eyes. I tried to laugh when I talked about running around like crazy for the bad sound movie when this person was in the hospital. He shook his head.

"I tried to get her to lay off." He said but he said it so softly as if the words would stick to the wall and he would get caught talking against 'the Head Cheerleader'.

"It's all good," I assured him and sipped the beer. "We're a team, right?" I smiled.

"Damn right, girl." He said, softly, and toasted me. Then he got up and hugged me tight for a long minute. He was all but clinging to me. I closed my eyes until he stopped shaking.

It was the best beer I have ever had in my life.

Moses.

I don't remember the moment I met Moses but I remember the first moment he made me feel special. It was a talent he had. He would find a damsel in distress and rescue them. He did that with anyone who needed just about anything. I would say he was the original 'give you the shirt off his back' guy.

This was Moses. He was raised in New Mexico, one of three kids, by a school janitor. His family didn't have a lot of money so they lived near the school in a house provided by the district and helped their dad clean the place they took social studies and algebra. There was no time to be a kid. It was all studies and hard work. So, naturally, as soon as he could, he rebelled.

A hard-drinking lifestyle and flesh skillfully colored with tattoos led him to become a bartender. A good one. One in demand. He also was a very talented guitar player. He and some friends formed a band and before they knew it they were touring the globe on the small circuit. He had success on his own terms. Once he returned home and the music group took a downturn, he opened a bar. He was the rowdy party boy on the outside but with a true heart of gold and an optimistic outlook on the life he made for himself. A real self-made man.

When you travel the music/bartending/tattooed road, you meet the fringe of society AKA porn stars. Through a friend of a friend Moses and Cynthia ended up at the same party and it was love at first sight. I'd watched Cynthia go through several painful heart aches and once she met Moses, she truly smiled from within. It was lovely to watch. However, Moses' family disowned him when they found out he was dating a porn star and it broke his heart every day. Never mind the head-to-toe tattoos and bartender work. Never mind the heavy drinking or partying around the world. All that was okay but a porn star? Nope. Mother, father, and siblings cut off all contact. Cynthia and Moses tried to hide the fact that she was a porn star from his family at first by saying she was in the music business. Seems they even had dinner at the family home and she tossed around something about MTV while being (as usual) glued to her phone. But the internet told a different story of her real work. Moses has a younger brother. They have wifi. It was pretty easy to put the pieces together. When he did talk about his family to me his eyes would rest on the floor and his voice was low and sad. He would look back up at me with such naked pain it hurt to look at. He would eventually shrug it off and say: "But, I'm living the life!" His smile would return but it would take a few minutes to become completely bright.

The moment Moses glowed in my eyes was a loud night at the Roxy in Hollywood. It was the release party for the Beach Blanket Slasher Parody. The edited trailer I had finished that day ran on a loop throughout the evening on the venue's walls. It was early still and the tiny space seemed empty. I felt completely exposed as this older person who just walked up to the Cool Kids table at lunch.

The Cheer Squad girls I saw were already in performance mode. I was met with quick hugs and left to my own devices. This was normal but that night I needed the shield of 'someone who belonged there' to give me legitimacy. I often sat with these girls on the set for hours and I heard all about their lives and loves and troubles back home. I became a confidante. But, out in the real world when they had to be 'on', I was in the way.

That's how I felt by the time Moses and Cynthia showed up. I was stuck in a half-circle booth enduring music so loud my ears would ring for days. Once they got there, I knew I could claim a headache and slip out and leave the Cool Kids to their drinks and partying. Moses walked in behind Cynthia and I watched him shake hands and say hi to people with a genuine smile. He spotted me and seemed a little shocked but very happy I was there. He hugged me tight like a long-lost friend.

"Hey girl, you made it! Let me get you a drink, no no don't you move. I got you. What are you drinking?" He asked, his mouth close to my ear like a good bartender who knew the sound of the place made it impossible to hear.

I instantly felt calm, and welcomed, as if I belonged.

Thanks to Moses I stayed for more of the night. I was lucky enough to hear a band I ended up liking. I was lucky enough to sit with people I had worked hard with on this movie and I was included. Moses made that happen. I have often felt out of place in the adult world no matter how much posturing I exuded. He made me feel like I was meant to be there.

When we shot at Cynthia's house, he became the Production Assistant's go-to guy. When Cynthia said jump, Moses said 'how high'. It worked for them. When her requests came fast and furious he would only smirk that crooked smile at me and say: "Anything for the Head Cheerleader, right?" I would laugh and of course, agree. We were all on the same team and Cynthia was driving the ship. Everyone did anything that needed to be done.

Each month I was handed footage for the web scenes. Along with the usual boy/girl often there was a blow job scene. Nothing special, just Cynthia and a POV (point of view) camera. Basically, the camera was the eyes of the viewer. The cameraman/male performer would hold the camera and Cynthia would act into it and often I could tell the male performer by their voice or body. I started to watch that month's footage and got this weird chill. I knew that voice. It was Moses holding the camera. I knew the black work of that stomach tattoo. That was Moses. I saw more of Moses than I ever planned and watched Cynthia and Moses have sex. You never saw Moses' face as he held the camera the whole time. This was before he was in Cynthia's movies. That story is next.

It was intimate. Not porn. I felt like I was intruding. But I also knew that for the POV Cynthia wouldn't have to pay a performer. Money saved, as she said. I got used to seeing Moses' talents on screen from the waist down. Still, he didn't change. He was still warm and wonderful. Once other companies realized it was Moses, they contacted Cynthia constantly to film with him. This was a fact Cynthia mentioned a lot. It was like throwing a piece of red meat into a piranha tank and everyone wanted a hunk of Moses. But, he was adamant. He was only doing POV and only with Cynthia.

The inevitable happened. I was downtown one night at a sketchy loft apartment nestled in an equally sketchy warehouse that was manufacturing pinatas on another floor. I was waiting for Cynthia and another girl to finish a scene that was going to be included in the monthly website offerings. Manzie, Cynthia's stills guy, was filming (saving money here) and Moses was nearby narrating as he always did during POVs. I settled into a chair I made sure I wouldn't stick to, took out my Nintendo 3DS, and waited.

Moses was still talking to the two girls as they moved to a couch. He was right next to Manzie so his voice would be on the camera then I noticed something odd. Moses was only in his underwear. I assumed he had been an off-camera plaything between scenes and it was none of my business. But the girls were beckoning him to join them. Of course, he said he shouldn't and his voice was shy and playful. Then it happened and my heart stopped. He stepped in front of the camera to join the girls on the couch. He was naked in seconds as the girls pounced on him. I stopped breathing. My mind was screaming *'NO! NO! COME BACK! You don't know how this works!'* I've never wanted to save someone so badly in my life. I had images of rushing the set, grabbing him by the wrist, and pulling him from the room. Later, he would sip hot tea while wrapped in a blanket, he would be unable to meet my eye, while I stroked his back and told him everything was okay. More like chug whiskey hiding under the bed as I set out full shot glasses to coax him back out to the real world.

Not so much, of course.

I watched the scene in abject horror and cried a few silent tears. Yes, I cried. I knew it was the beginning of the end of the Moses. But maybe he would buck the system? Maybe he would avoid becoming a porn douchebag? Maybe… maybe…

I cried again when I edited the scene. No one knows that. To this day it was probably the hardest editing I've ever had to do.

Once Cynthia had him in front of the camera, other studios insisted on using him. But, Moses would only do it if Cynthia approved of the girl he was to work with and the amount of money he would get. She wasn't his agent but she acted like one. He was new to the business, it wasn't a bad thing. She protected him.

Months later, I was on their back porch during a shoot at Cynthia's house between scenes. Moses came back from a shoot with another company, exhausted, and flopped into a chair grabbing a beer. He downed half of it then let out a big breath.

"Rough day?" I asked with a small laugh. He laughed and nodded.

"No shit. I was up at 9 am for this shoot and I'm just home now!" He said, exasperated. It was nearly 10 pm. "It was only one scene!" He laughed.

"Damn. Can I get you anything? You hungry?" I asked, half sitting up and prepared to grab what he needed then happily listen to his day. He was about to answer with a small shake of his head when the sliding glass door opened and Cynthia poked her head out.

"Hey, come here a minute." She said offhandedly to Moses, eyes on her phone, and she disappeared back into the house, barely meeting his eyes. The man was out of his chair like a shot. The bottle of beer all but spun on its axis before it settled on the table.

As a couple, they shared everything. Living space etc. The money that Moses made doing scenes for other directors, Cynthia called it his 'hooker' money. I knew it was a joke but I watched Moses hand it over more than once. All the finances were in her hands. From rent to utilities to credit card bills. This included Moses' 'hooker' money. I once heard her in an interview laugh about how old-fashioned Moses was as he was trying to squire money away to buy her an engagement ring. She laughed when she figured out what he was doing. He was trying to be his old-fashioned romantic self. As the former Moses peeked out, she laughed as if it was the stupidest thing ever. Not a cute girly adorable laugh, a mocking one. She laughs at things she doesn't understand like a mean girl in a high school cafeteria.

He performed in just about every Cynthia movie, of course, for free. Then, he would work in other director's projects. Then, he would do music, and trailers, cook food for the cast and crew as well as be the set's PA. I watched him start to crumble over the next few months.

He began to hang out with Dane. Dane was a very popular male performer and his star was just starting to rise and Cythina used him a lot. One thing Dane wasn't allowed to do on other sets was be mean to his female co-star. No slapping or name-calling. In Cynthia's scenes, she let it happen. I watched it happen a little here and there and when he and Moses would tag team a girl together, it happened more. I watched Moses begin to slap the girls more and talk more derogatoryly about them or their parts. This was an act for the camera, I am sure. If not, maybe it was his true douche self starting to form in the wake of working with Dane. Either way, his performing style changed and I noticed it in the raw footage.

The drinking was always there but he never ever performed drunk or high. Ever. He was always a professional in that respect. Whenever I came to the house for a shoot, he always greeted me warmly as he did that first night at the Hollywood club. I would be invited to take shots of whatever alcohol he was enjoying that night and I did. As an older female, closer to the age of the performer's mother, it always astonished people that I drank. As if I was some evil soccer mom. I didn't drink much but a shot or two over the eight-hour shoot and I was in the club. As Moses worked more, the hugs became less. The warm hello's become less frequent. I could see the cracks in the man widen. I would walk in and get a simple: "Hey Sonny." from Moses as he rushed from one task to the next. If he had a split second, I might get a kiss on the cheek but those evaporated just as quickly.

When I was let go after four years, Cynthia cried. She cried as she fired me even as I offered solutions to her money issues by lowering my rate etc. But, by this time, Moses was handling everything. It was pretty much let him edit for free rather than pay an outside editor. I helped them organize everything when I returned the hard drives.

The day I dropped off the multiple hard drives, he helped me with the boxes. There were about 20 hard drives and a box of old tapes. He looked over the electronic pile and I watched him go white as a sheet. This was real and all his responsibility now. She was going to lean on him the way she had leaned on me but worse. He was going to be a full-time editor, graphic artist, musician, performer, and production assistant. As well as still running his bar in New Mexico. He would wistfully talk about his family whom he missed desperately then when emotion would rise up, he would dismiss it quickly and smile.

"I'm living the life though, right?" He would say and usually high-five Dane. But that smile? It wasn't a smile I knew. I now know the meaning of 'a smile that never reached his eyes'. I'd seen this look on many a porn star in my career. It broke my heart every time.

Cynthia cried when she fired me more because she said she was going to miss me. I assured her we would still be friends and this was only business. I had a deeper opinion but why burn that bridge? That's a different chapter in this book. I knew more than anything I was going to miss Moses. I remember the night I heard they were getting married. My partner and I had been invited to stay for dinner at their home after a shoot, which in itself was rare, but it was nice to be included. Cynthia sat at the island in the kitchen and very succinctly mapped out their Vegas wedding that was going to happen on Valentine's Day the following year. I looked up as I caught the conversation and blinked.

"Wait, you are really getting married?" I asked.

"Yeah, in Vegas." She said offhandedly, not pleased I had interrupted.

But I had heard no story of a proposal or didn't see a ring. Either way, I was so happy for them I wept a few tears. She laughed at me. Laughed. At. Me. That cool mocking laugh. I wasn't invited to the wedding. It was after I had been let go.

The following January, after the wedding, I made my way to Las Vegas for the AVN Convention. By this time, I had landed on my feet and secured a good job at a mainstream content management company. I was retiring from adult slowly. The last time I was at AVN the Cheer Squad booth was huge! Several tables were strewn with merchandise and a massive canopy covered the area with the company logo emblazoned on it. It was a party spot and everyone stopped and smiled and partied.

This year, there were only two tables, no canopy, and a banner tacked on the wall that sagged in several places. It was exposed and looked cheap. Cynthia herself looked gaunt and tired. Moses was distracted.

"Hey." I smiled.

"Oh hey, girl." He said, half smiling, kissing my cheek, snapping gum as he looked around the room. Later I found out he was looking for Dane. His new best friend.

Several of the girls were genuinely happy to see me and it felt good to be missed. One girl hugged me super tight and then made sure she caught my eye.

"Things are different, man." She whispered up at me since she was about 5 feet tall. "Like, really tense."

"Was getting that way before I was let go," I whispered back and she hugged me tight again.

"It's bad. She shouldn't have let you go. I'm worried about him." She sighed. I heard those words from just about every Cheer Squad girl. *I'm worried about him.* We all knew who we meant. I glanced at Moses who smiled across the room as Dane came into view and the two of them hugged. Once Dane arrived, it seemed the party started.

I left the group with a smile and did a few more laps. When I circled back to their booth, I noticed Moses was gone and the girls that were there looked miserable and bored. I made my way to the AVN Autograph Row and spotted Dane and I knew Moses would be close by. I stopped to talk to them then Dane slipped away to meet someone else and I looked up at Moses.

"How's it going?" I asked with a smile.

"It's going." He shrugged, looking after Dane and chewing gum again. He met my eyes and smiled a little.

"You don't look happy," I said quietly. He just shook his head as if he wanted to speak but couldn't.

"Not crazy about doing this but Cynthia sort of said I was doing it." He confessed as he kept looking over my head to see who was around. I also knew that if you signed at the AVN booth, you got paid. Cynthia was whoring him out for money blatantly.

"It's not too bad. You got Dane." I said and he smiled a little.

"It was something I insisted on. If I had to do this for two hours, I was doing it with Dane or not at all." He said, fingers tapping the DVD cases he was going to sign for fans. I spotted the title and sighed a little. I hadn't edited this one; it was brand new.

"Remind me to get one of those from Cynthia when I get paid." I half-joked, knowing if I wanted one I could get it but I would, of course, offer her money.

Without hesitation, he slid the case across the table at me.

"Here." He said.

"You sure?"

"Oh yeah, I'm sure." He said, only a little bitterness in his voice, his eyes still scanning the room. Once Dane showed back up he was all smiles and they retreated to the back of the signing booth.

"Okay, see ya," I said and slipped the case into my bag.

"See ya." He said and went back to his conversation. I felt dismissed. Pushed aside. The douchebag takeover was happening.

The next story I heard about Moses sealed the deal. He had been hired to be part of a gang bang and on the day of the shoot, Cynthia called the director.

"I know his rate is $500 but for this, he is going to need $600." She said.

The director was dumbfounded and then assured her he had already signed the papers and agreed to the price.

When he showed up, this particular director made everyone sign something that said they wouldn't put anything out on social media about the scene until the scene was released. It's a smart move as everyone indulges in social media with every aspect of their life.

On the set and during the scene, Moses took out his phone and did a monetized Snap Chat to the Cheer Squad viewers making money on someone else's set for Cynthia's company. He talked about the girl he was going to bang and when the scene was done, showed more video of the aftermath. During the scene, he was also rough with the girl, slapping her face, etc. which is something this director frowned upon but could not get him to stop. Needless to say, the director never hired him again. This is not the only story I've heard like this and when it is repeated, stories about him are not refuted. Moses' Douche Bag Reputation has been solidified.

I still tear up as I write this. I watched this super sweet thoughtful guy become a douchebag porn star in the span of two years. He and Cynthia have married and I truly hope he is happy. They've launched a clothing line together. Well, in Cynthia's latest interview, she said: "I've launched a new clothing line." Not 'we'. Just her. She didn't include Moses.

She finally let me go in 2016. On Valentine's Day. Over the phone. Crying.

I knew she was downsizing but on the down low, I got the backstory. She had been on the phone in the backyard when the doorbell rang. Moses went to answer it. At the door were three men in suits from OSHA. They wanted to come in and take pictures. What are OSHA Violations? An OSHA violation occurs when a company or employee willingly or unknowingly ignores potential and real safety hazards. Like, not using condoms for a shoot, it was still a thing. So, surprise inspections happened if they knew you were shooting porn.

"Yeah, sure dudes. C'mon in." Moses said. Smiling. Cynthia never used a permit to film and someone had ratted her out. She was fined over $100,000.

Remember the 'you have a job for life' line? Yeah, neither did she.

When things got tough in porn and the internet was having its way with all of us, I did my best to stick to my guns and not drop my price like everyone else had.

I was charging what I was worth after so many years in school and then in the practical world of post-production, At least I didn't raise my price!

After Cynthia, I shopped myself around for more work. I would go into the meetings all happy and ready to tackle the work and then the money came up and the dark clouds would gather.

"Wow, your price is a bit much, Can you come down on that?" The director would swirl his bourbon in his glass. My price hadn't changed in years and he knew that. This was just the dance we did in negotiations and he was ready to step on my toes, hard. We'd be meeting at a bar, usually. Food was sometimes involved but that meant we'd have to have a real conversion.

"My price is my price," I said but the foundation on my upper lip was cracking and I felt the job slipping away.

"Kind of out of my budget." The director would sip and sigh sadly as if I was his only hope and he'd have to sell his dog to afford me. Poor Fido. Out in the cold, probably in the rain, because I wouldn't budge. "And it will take you no time at all to edit. It's an easy shoot." And now he's selling the kids into child labor. All because of me.

I did my best, I honestly did. I would explain it like this:

Time, quality, and price. You will only ever and I mean ever get two. Do you want it fast and cheap? The quality will probably suffer. You want to pay less but want it on time. The quality WILL suffer. Do you want high quality in half the time? My price just doubled. See?

After explaining it to the director I would drop my price anyway and regret it all the way home. Not to mention I would think I was getting paid promptly. However, after any changes from him, changes from the studio, changes from the blonde in the feature who hates her left ass cheek and can I please cut it out every time it's on-screen? I would not get that final check for months after I said yes. Long after I needed that or any money. I needed to be more smart about business.

My last mistake... Um.. porn job.. was Godzilla.

I have a full-time tech job now in the mainstream and porn is the sideline. Or was. Or might still be. Either way, I was on a new path. I had asked the Universe for guidance and it gave it to me. Happily, I went down the mainstream road. Yet, this side street of porn was calling. It led to the usual back alley of what I believed was easy cash. Or so I thought.

I answered an ad online for a company looking for editors. I figured the extra cash would be nice when eventually I would be paid, so I applied. Soon, I was contacted and a Skype interview was set up. I was in California, this company was in Canada.

On the small screen were two young people, a female, and a male. Nice looking kids. They liked my resume and wanted to know more.

"Tell us about your editing experience?" The girl asked in earnest. Then, I did something I thought I would never do. I would like to credit Shelly Winters for this one. When she went to her auditions and they asked for her credentials, she would plop her Oscar awards on their desk and just smile.

"Oh okay," I said. I stood and grabbed my AVN Hall of Fame award and plopped it in front of me so it took up the whole screen. They were quiet for a minute.

"Oh... that really is you." She said.

"Yep."

"Okay, so we can send out some contracts on Monday. Can you talk to our tech guy here about specs?" She said and closed her portfolio. I had the job.

The kids were nice but they were trying to re-invent the porn wheel. I've seen it before. They think they are doing something SO groundbreaking! It's people having sex, kids. Relax. They shot on three cameras (I still think that's redundant, my opinion only) and had their own text package and music. Honestly, it was a streamlined job and they liked my editing. As usual, starts out great.

I was still at the day job but stressing very hard about this freelance stuff. The back alley to easy cash was starting to be strewn with land mines.

After a few months, their directors started shooting with a different camera setting. It was all the rage and the new thing therefore like most porn places they jumped on it. It was to prove they could be cutting-edge. It will soon (and has) died out. When one place does a new thing, they all have to do it. I went from an editor to an editor/colorist. I do not do color. It's something that has been happening in porn as well as the mainstream. You might think you are only an editor but the laundry list of things most productions ask you to do makes you a one-man band. It's cheaper for the production and someone will do it if you say no. They will find some wide-eyed kid to jump up without question. So, you do it.

I managed the first scene or two just fine but then I got one scene that was so off, making it all match color-wise was just insane. Usually, we had 2 or 3 revisions but this one went to 9.

The next thing I know I am back on another Skype call.

"How can we make this work for you?" The girl asked. It became a millennial kumbaya fest of 'How are we feeling?' and offering me avocado toast and pear kombucha. I found myself down the same dark 'love me and I can do anything' road. I cried a lot. I felt useless and angry. I lost sleep at the uselessness of it. I made mistakes at the day job.

I had seen the clear road yet taken the back alley strewn with broken glass. Gleefully, I had taken off my shoes and was prancing through it. I ignored the pain and the blood and my crying. It was what I had been used to for over 25 years.

Then the Universe spoke up.

"Hey! What are you doing?" It asked in its booming voice.

"Going down this path of broken glass barefoot." I sniveled.

"I showed you the good path. The one where people respect you and you have health insurance." It said. "Don't you like that path?"

"I love that path. I am used to this one." I said, looking at my wounds and feeling helpless. Then the Universe took my hand and showed me the other path again. It was like training a blind person who had just gotten their sight. The other path had people who respected me and my talent. People who accepted me for who I am which is something I had never felt in porn. I quit Godzilla and began to heal. It was a long hard road but I felt free.

CHAPTER FOURTEEN

After all I had been through that year with Cynthia firing me and Godzilla trying to fake care, it was as if the Universe slipped a hand over me and stroked my hair gently saying "That'll do, pig. That'll do." Yes, I was thinking of the movie Babe. If I told that anecdote and someone laughed, I knew they got it.

When it came time for AVN in January again, I had spent the previous months agonizing about going. This was an annual ritual: should I go, would anyone notice, did I care? When a mainstream friend came up with a free suite for me and anyone I wanted to bring, I really could not say no. My best friend and I drove out through a pounding rainstorm that almost had me driving back and we landed in Vegas. The normal four-hour trip took six. I had comp passes to the trade show and a comp ticket to the award show: the perks of being a Hall of Famer.

After I freshened up, my friend and I hit the trade show floor. As usual, I didn't take three steps without someone coming up and hugging me. I would introduce my friend and we walked on.

I had been going to this show for over 10 years or more and for the first time, I wasn't wearing the rose-colored desperation glasses. The gloss was gone and what I saw were little booths and too young girls dressed too skimpily leaning over to passing men and smiling like it was a whore house in the red light of Amsterdam. It simply seemed tawdry. I'm the one who always walked in like I owned the place and knew everyone and was everyone's friend. Now when I told people I was working in mainstream they looked at me in awe. As if I had just tunneled out of Alcatraz with a plastic dessert spoon.

I made my way around the show floor and saw Moses grumbling at the AVN booth waiting for Dane. But you know that story.

Next to him was Stone Brooke. He is a very prominent black performer I had worked for years before and he always was a gentleman to me. He was in the middle of an interview and I slipped past as not to bother him when I felt his large hand on my shoulder.

"C'mere girl." He said with a deep voice and pulled me into a tight hug.

"I didn't want to bother you," I said, smiling and hugging him back.

"You never bother me. Drink later?" He said and let me go with a nod and went back to his interview without a break.

I later emailed him and thanked him for always being such a gentleman to me. That lasted 4 months as I emailed him later about a project he had his usual editor work on for him. I emailed to offer my help if he needed it since I heard it had a lot of special effects and seemed like a big project. I was letting him know I was still open to freelance. I was wishing him well and offering a hand. He told me to check myself and he had chosen this editor for this project and that was that. The gentleman had become a porn douchebag person once again.

The rest of the show had that same sheen of stripper sweat and watered-down drinks.

The night of the AVN awards, I flew solo and met my friends inside. I walked the red carpet and stood for the photographers I knew, smiling and posing. The ones that didn't know me could have cared less and I was fine with it. Once inside, I got a drink and looked for a place to sit. People seemed happy to see me and the party talk was pleasant. I wore a cross-body purse I never took off. Never made that mistake again!

I heard all the usual 'let's meet up back in LA' lines from more than a dozen people. I am just as much to blame, I never called them either. Normally when I get home I spend days calling the directors and companies whose cards I'd managed to wrangle. I did anything to get work. But this year, I had a day job with benefits and things looked very different.

CHAPTER FIFTEEN

#lifeafterporn

When I fell out of porn, or rather it pushed me from the plane without a parachute, my partner and I decided to try a fresh start. We slimmed down our belongings and decided to move near family in South Carolina. I had three mainstream jobs lined up and we had a place to live. We packed up the truck and drove cross country to start over.

Once we got there, the humidity hit us like a brick and the jobs dried up within days. Each job saying 'We are restructuring, talk to us in six months'. We lasted two and a half weeks. No lie. A quick call to our previous landlord and we moved back to the same house we had just left in Los Angeles. Our neighbor still had our keys.

When we came back to California, leaving Road Runner-like skid marks all across the 40, I had a singular focus: a steady job.

Of course, before we left, I was offered a position at another mid-size porn house. They were going through a restructuring and were adding an edit bay. It would be the exact same position I held at PornTown and I would be paid the exact same money (or close to it, possibly less) as I was at PornTown twenty-plus years before. I turned it down because we were packed and ready to leave. Once porn kicked me in the head for the last time (Cynthia letting me go) I thought moving out of town was the thing to do! Was it a mistake? I just knew that porn path and that path was nothing but pain and stress all the way down the road and I was done with it. It was one of the hardest things I have ever done. I would even have been working with a very dear friend I had lost touch with. But I said no.

Footnote here: When I got back I went to an Adult Industry mixer and met one of the guys who had been present in my interview. Seems the company's owner's brother had swooped in and made some drastic changes. I would have lost my job within a month. So, bullet dodged.

I became laser-focused on mainstream. I wanted a job that would be steady and maybe have a benefit or two. Within a month, I had three interviews. Even that startled me! One company offered me the job over the phone because they loved my personality and my qualifications. Also, someone who already worked there recommended me. That person was Ross from my Old Guard days! I went to the other two job interviews but they could not meet the money I was offered so I went with the first tech company. It turned out to be a graveyard shift which completely threw me. But, my partner is amazing (i.e.: making sure the bedroom was blacked out, making sure I ate) and we made it work for 7 months before I moved to swing shift.

But I go too fast here, I want to back up.

On my first day at the new job, I was welcomed with open arms. I promised the guy that interviewed me over the phone donuts if I got hired. On my first day, I arrived with a dozen and he purposely left a meeting just to meet me. He was shocked but happy that I brought them! Sadly, he was only here to fill a few positions then he was moving on. I got his number before he left.

Within a few days, I felt more at home at this new company than I ever had in porn in 25 years. People asked about me. Smiled at me. Welcomed me. It was a whole new experience. I still had a foot in porn with a couple of freelance clients so I didn't feel totally out of the business. Also, the new place knew of my porn background and had no problem with it. This company processes softcore porn for a few places in town. I giggled when I had to sign something that said I was okay seeing porn on the job. Actually, I laughed for a solid ten minutes.

With everyone knowing my background, some co-workers wanted to get the 'in' at the local porn star karaoke watering hole just down the street in Burbank. It was one of the IT guy's birthday so they called ahead and got a large table for the night. The party headed over after their shift ended at 6 pm but I worked until midnight. I was getting constant texts from 9 pm on telling me to join them and they were waiting for their turn to sing to come up but it was so busy. I eventually caved and left work early. I walked in and was of course greeted as I always was, by name and with hugs. This happened about every five feet as I walked to the large table. I looked at my new co-workers and their mouths were hanging open. I had just proven that I did indeed know these people. They had been, what I thought had been, my tribe. One female co-worker had noticed a male performer she recognized and she asked if he knew 'Madison'. He didn't. When she brought him to the table, he smiled wide. "Oh, Sonny!" He laughed and greeted me warmly. We had known each other for over twenty years and he never knew my real name. Rather the norm in porn. I went to the Karaoke host, Nikki. (She of the motor boar introduction at Old Guard.) and got a long hug and kiss. I told her where I was working now and indicated my new crew at the large table. Within minutes, my new tribe had all their songs being played and the birthday boy got a faux lap dance from Nikki herself.

Sadly, Local Karaoke was not to last. It had been in existence for thirteen years and the owner just could not make the business work anymore. Times had changed. He was losing the lease. On the very last night, my new tribe wanted to go but knew they had to get there early to get in. They went over around 7 pm. One of my co-workers waited to go over with me. When we arrived, the line to get in stretched around the building. I hugged the owner, grabbed my co-worker's hand and we walked right in. He also didn't believe that I knew everyone there. We didn't make it ten feet into the building before I was greeted with hugs and smiles. Of course, two of my male co-workers spotted some very pretty young girls. I, of course, knew them and handled the introductions. It's what I do. I am the perfect wingman.

Looking back, it's amazing how often I was hugged and greeted yet still did not feel like a part of the porn community. I wonder if it's just something we needed in porn; touching without a paycheck. Human contact without a binding contract.

I kept that one foot in porn my first year in the mainstream job. I still went to parties and events and worked in porn. I found myself still craving that porn approval and when I got it, it was almost like a high. If I got praise or once I got a card at Christmas from a new porn company I was working with and I could have framed it. It made me giddy. Which is why when things went wrong, I took it even harder.

Yet, when things went wrong at the mainstream place, I was told "Hey, it's okay. Here's how to do it." and it was done. It was like some sort of dream to have that level of common respect.

When things went south with Godzilla I was told in the end that the QC person was over-qualified for his job therefore the blame was solely on me. If I had listed even half of the mainstream companies I had worked and was currently working with, I would have just been bragging rather than trying to put them in their place. I never did tell them. It wasn't worth it. In the end, I still found myself reaching for them. Begging for that approval. When I got the final payment I apologized again as if it was some sort of Hail Mary. I was told no bridges were burned and it was all good. I have to be content with that.

I went to the day job the next day in an odd mood. Out of place. I had been paid and I was out of porn. Porn Free. I'd been editing porn since 1991 and here it was 2018 and… no porn. I didn't know it would hit me so hard or mess with my head so much. I had been Sonny Malone for so many years I felt like I had to reinvent myself but I didn't. I just had to be me and 'me' was either laughed at or ignored for years in porn. At the new job, I didn't have to reinvent myself or bend myself to please anyone. For the first time in my life, I could be who I wanted to be without recrimination or judgment. I had the time and space to figure out who I was.

I had been at the day job for over a year now and thought I was still 'the porn chick' but I wasn't. I was in my head but to everyone at work I was simply 'Madison'. I had made that my name for a reason; to be whoever I wanted. It took me this long to begin to fit into that name. I still get this shock when I see my name in the system at the day job because it takes me a minute to realize; that's *me*.

I was having quite the pity party for myself when a coworker in another department that I had become friends with (and was at my wedding years later) messaged me on interoffice Skype:

Suzanne 7:48 PM:
Hiiii!
Madison 7:48 PM:
hi ;) what's up?
Suzanne 7:48 PM:
totally not work-related
Madison 7:48 PM:
oh okay
Suzanne 7:48 PM:
April 26th after your shift? Are you free?
Madison 7:49 PM:
I could be
Suzanne 7:49 PM:
you'll have to be
Madison 7:49 PM:
why is that? cause the 27th is my birthday?
Suzanne 7:49 PM:
(chuckle)
Madison Premo 7:49 PM:
LOL
Suzanne 7:50 PM:
come over here later when u get a chance. we'll discuss the details

This is normal for my day job. My birthday was celebrated by the entire department with cake and Chinese food. Then Suzanne took me out for drinks after our shift! When I had my first anniversary at the day job, I was given congrats all around. I have never felt more welcomed at a job in my life.

Another way I was shoved out the porn door: I knew that Lincoln was going through a divorce, sadly, and his wife had been the editor on 90% of his projects. They had to keep money coming into the house and she was a former mainstream editor. When I saw the breakup happen, on Twitter no less, I messaged Linc:

> 'Hey! I just saw what you're going through. If you need anything, let me know. I can pick up any editing if you need a hand in the meantime.'

No response.

But, his next Tweet:

"Hey, all! Meet my new editor! The most amazing guy ever!" with a link to the guy's Twitter.

Kicked in the teeth by porn again.

When I did try to take on a project from Linc, sadly it would not work. My system was too old at that point since I no longer do any freelance. But I sat there, trying anyway, and felt sick as I went down that same path of digitizing, seeing what needed to be edited, waiting for the inevitable phone call of 'Man we got a problem'. Not to mention for the amount of work I was going to have to do, I was being offered less than a third of my price. Around one thousand. I never should have said yes in the first place but I was hoping for that last connection that maybe I could be a friend and save the day. I was completely fooling myself. I was grabbing behind me for a life that was so gone it wasn't even in my rearview mirror anymore.

Knowing porn people can give one that sense of celebrity. I know famous people even if they are on the fringe of society. I find myself talking about the industry and people look at me like I'm some sort of expert. I am not a celebrity. Fighting the need to prove my worth in this world is something I still struggle with.

This is where I leave you. I have changed (almost) every name and indeed left out some folks for my own reasons. I still have porn friends and can still get a drink at any porn function. At the new job, I make any new hire handle the monthly porn work. My dance card is full.

END

www.ingramcontent.com/pod-product-compliance
Lightning Source LLC
Chambersburg PA
CBHW050342160726
48002CB00001B/421